ELVIS, WILLIE, JESUS & ME

Smyth & Helwys Publishing, Inc.
6316 Peake Road
Macon, Georgia 31210-3960
1-800-747-3016
©2008 by Smyth & Helwys Publishing

The paper used in this publication meets the minimum requirements of
American National Standard for Information Sciences—
Permanence of Paper for Printed Library Materials.
ANSI Z39.48–1984. (alk. paper)
Cover art by Greg Cravens

Library of Congress Cataloging-in-Publication Data

Montgomery, Bert.

Elvis, Willie, Jesus, and me : the musings and mutterings of a
church misfit / by Bert Montgomery. p. cm.
ISBN 978-1-57312-521-5 (pbk. : alk. paper)
1. Popular culture—Religious aspects—Christianity.
I. Title. BR115.C8M647
2008 286.1'092—dc22 [B] 2008038334

Elvis, Willie, Jesus, and Me

The Musings and Mutterings of a Church Misfit

Bert Montgomery

Dedication

For Jency, Rob, and Daniel,
who have had to put up with my
existential angst for far too long,
and without whom I'd have been
a goner long, long ago.
This book should be called
Elvis, Willie, Jesus, Jency, Rob, Daniel, and Me . . .
but that seemed just a tad too long.

Acknowledgments

Giving Thanks . . .

Jeremy Samples, editor with Smyth & Helwys Publishing, is in charge of the online community Caleb's Café (www.calebscafe.com). Jeremy took an interest in my writing and gave me total freedom (well, *almost*) to write many of these pieces for the Café.

Thanks also to Mike Smith, Michael Duncan, David Adams, Glenn Hinson, Tex Sample, and Daniel Bailey for encouraging me to write and write often, and for always providing helpful feedback. Thanks to everyone who is in any way associated with the Baptist Seminary of Kentucky (www.bsky.org), especially Drs. Greg Earwood and Dalen Jackson (president and dean, respectively), for a progressive, seminary-as-formation approach that allowed this ADD-gifted nut to thrive. And, thanks to my fellow BSK-ers, Amanda, Brandy, Charlie, Patsey, and Sonny, who helped me survive my third attempt at a seminary education.

Greg Cravens, Memphis artist extraordinaire, deserves thanks for capturing the essence of my work in his illustrations. Greg, I'm sorry it didn't all work out this time, but thanks for the cover!

Thanks to Mom, Dad, and sister Becky for putting up with my eccentricities and giving me room to grow, but with needed boundaries; and to Jency, Rob, and Daniel for enduring my erratic writing habits and all the time I take to write, and for loving me anyway. (Jency has been telling me to write for a long, long time, but I'm a slow listener.)

And to the churches that have nurtured me, encouraged me, and challenged me—First Baptist, Norco, Louisiana; Northside Baptist, Clinton, Mississippi; Second Baptist, Memphis, Tennessee; First United Methodist, Henderson, Kentucky; Melbourne Heights Baptist, Louisville, Kentucky; Campbellsburg Baptist, Campbellsburg, Kentucky; and now the good folks at University

Baptist at Mississippi State University—a congregation that knows what it's NOT, calling a pastor who knows what he's NOT, in hopes that God will form us all into what we can BE.

Thanks to everyone who has been a part of my journey in some way or another to this point.

Laissez les bons temps rouler!

Contents

Prologue

(Or, What's This All About?)

Several years ago I was asked to write a book. Actually, I was *told* I *had* to write a book . . . sort of. Don't you just hate that? It's bad enough being in school and being told you have to *read* certain books! However, in order to earn a master's degree in sociology, I had to *write* a thesis, which was then bound in a hard, black cover, catalogued, and placed in the Mississippi College library. That's kind of like writing a book, isn't it? Don't worry. This is a very different kind of book than my master's thesis (however, if for some bizarre reason you are into that type of thing, my thesis is on the college library shelves there in Clinton, Mississippi).

Unlike the long, grueling, pseudo-academic treatise that preceded it, *Elvis, Willie, Jesus, and Me* is a collection of short observations and reflections on life, society, faith, and church, with a rock-and-roll attitude. I *chose* to write this, just as you are *choosing* to read it. I think of it as being like a big pot of journalistic jambalaya with healthy doses of Mike Royko, Anne Lamott, Lewis Grizzard, Will Campbell, J. K. Rowling, and Bugs Bunny all mixed together. These reflections and observations cover everything from pain and death to politics and finances, from cursing and sex and to prayer and family board games. Oh, and a whole lot about God, love, Jesus, and grace. Much of what is assembled here has appeared in print previously, primarily in Smyth & Helwys's online community, CalebsCafe.com; others on EthicsDaily.com; some also in *Baptists Today*, *The Wittenburg Door*, and even the Baton Rouge, Louisiana, newspaper, *The Advocate*.

Essentially, these observations and such are my way of trying to come to terms with life as I know it—primarily as I knew it between the years of 2002 and 2008, when I was beginning to get paid to be a "minister" and trying to complete seminary. Hopefully, somewhere in these mumblings, you may recognize glimpses of life, faith, church, God, death, Elvis, and yourself—glimpses of life as you know it, too. If not, the title of my thesis is *The* Verstehen *of Secularization and Schism: A Weberian Analysis of Southern Baptists' Orientation Toward Change.* Choose your reading, and go have fun.

Part 1
Beware the Odes of March!

My birthday is in March,
and these are my odes . . . plus a few other things.

Saint Willie

(Ode to Willie Nelson)

Thank God for Willie Nelson!

As I recover in bed after the skillful hands of a surgeon have removed about twelve inches of my colon, my spirit is being refreshed by the skillful voice and hands of a master musician. A short stack of favorite CDs lies next to the bed, but the one receiving the most play is Willie's 1978 classic, *Stardust.*

Funny, *Stardust* isn't even my favorite of Willie's albums. But there is something magical about it—all of those old pop standards, like "Georgia on My Mind," "Someone to Watch Over Me," and "On the Sunny Side of the Street." It is a joyous record that always lifts my spirits in a way that few others can.

I've also been reading some Thomas Merton. Merton writes in *The Seven Storey Mountain,* "It is a wonderful experience to discover a new saint. For God is greatly magnified and marvelous in each one of His saints: differently in each individual one. There are no two saints alike: but all of them are like God, like Him in a different and special way."[1]

Merton's saint was found in the Catholic tradition. Mine came from outside. I'm stating it right here and now: *Willie Nelson is a saint!*

You may question the subject matter of some of Willie's songs. You may point out some of Willie's personal habits. But I'm telling you—nobody, *nobody,* can sing "I'll Fly Away," "Uncloudy Day," or "Amazing Grace" with more gospel exuberance than Willie!

Maybe it's his honesty. There's no self-righteousness here—Willie is who he is. He doesn't hide his failures or habits from himself or anybody else. That's one reason Willie speaks to me: I wish I could be so transparent before God and others.

Maybe it's his activism. Willie freely speaks his mind about, and gets his hands dirty working on, the moral issues of the day: his work for family farmers in an age of corporate greed run amuck; his opinions and songs about war (present Iraq war included); his continued support of underdog political candidates who aren't owned by big-money interests.

Yes, Willie has a gut-level integrity and a strong moral compass that reflect the truth of the gospel. I only wish preachers (including me) would show such a moral compass and such personal integrity!

Whatever it may be, I can't really explain it. I am constantly brought into a spirit of joy and yes, into the very presence of God, when I listen to Willie Nelson.

I doubt any other Baptist preacher has ever declared someone a saint—especially someone usually considered quite the sinner. But there is *something* about Willie Nelson that reflects the love of God to me and into the world. In Merton's terms, there's *something* about Willie Nelson that is like God in a unique and special way.

So, here's to Saint Willie—the patron saint of rebels, outlaws, and exceptional sinners! Thanks be to God!

Note

[1] In my well-worn paperback edition, this is found on page 387 (that's the 1976 Harcourt Brace & Company edition out of San Francisco).

Life, Death, Community ... and *Scrubs*

(Ode to *Not* Being Superman)

Everything I've learned about life, death, and community I've learned from watching the TV show *Scrubs*. Well, that may not be exactly true, but *Scrubs*, simply put, is one of the best "Christian" shows on television.

If you've watched *Scrubs*, then you probably know what I mean. Or you may be wondering what a show filled with drinking, promiscuity, harassment, ridicule, God-mocking, sexual innuendo, bathroom humor, surreal visions, and the health-care system has to do with faith.

I'm no Bible scholar, but I haven't found any place in the Bible that defines what characteristics make a TV show "morally Christian" or "reprehensibly non-Christian." I'm also no moral theologian, but I have found that many of the greatest biblical stories are filled with drinking, promiscuity, harassment, ridicule, God-mocking, sexual innuendo, bathroom humor, surreal visions, and even health-care issues.

And I'm no TV producer, but I'm certain that a realistic telling of our great faith stories would be considered "reprehensibly non-Christian." Imagine *The Adventures of Abraham and Sarah*; *All in King David's Family*; *Desperate Housewives of King Solomon*; *My Name Is Jael*.

When I read the ancient scriptural stories of real people living in the real world, I recognize schoolmates, neighbors, bosses, colleagues, teachers, friends, enemies, and family members. Sometimes

I even recognize myself. Which brings me back to *Scrubs*—set in the fictitious Sacred Heart Hospital, it deals honestly with obesity, alcoholism, drug addiction, diabetes, infertility, unplanned pregnancy, parental responsibility, vocational calling, unpleasant working conditions, and even religion.

I love the characters: J.D., Elliot, Turk, Carla, Perry Cox, Bob Kelso, "the Todd," and the janitor. Each has personal strengths, and each has tremendous weaknesses. These doctors, nurses, and staff argue with each other over proper treatments for patients and whether or not surgery is necessary. They also encourage and challenge each other. They ridicule each other and play silly games with each other. Individually, while interacting together, they each are searching for meaning and purpose amid their chaotic lives.

Essentially, they are a bunch of well-trained screw-ups. They can do their jobs well, sometimes perfectly, but their inner lives and their relationships with others are a total mess. They unintentionally hurt each other, sometimes deeply; and they even *intentionally* hurt each other, sometimes deeply. Patients die of natural causes despite these medical professionals' best efforts. Patients are permanently scarred or even die because of one simple, little mistake made by a doctor or nurse.

We watch as family members appear and seize our affections, leaving us to grieve with and hurt for our favorite characters when those family members die. We watch when the characters—even occasionally the despicable ones—come through in support of a colleague at such critical times. We are made privy to the thoughts and reflections of hard, tough, and unpleasant life lessons learned. We watch a thirty-minute comedy and by the end of it we catch little glimpses of what life, death, and community are really about.

When I watch *Scrubs* I recognize schoolmates, neighbors, bosses, colleagues, teachers, friends, enemies, and family members. Sometimes I even recognize myself. Just like people you and I know—just like the people we read about in the Bible—J.D. and company are hard-living yet good people who simply can't make it on their own. They truly need each other. Which brings me to the theme song. If you know it, sing along: "I can't do this all on my own; No, I know I'm no Superman."[1]

And this is why *Scrubs* is one of the best "Christian" shows on television. After all, isn't this the essential message of the Scriptures? Isn't this the essential message of the Gospels? Isn't this essentially the message and meaning of the coming of Christ Jesus?

I can't do this all on my own; no, I know I'm no Superman.

Note

[1] The song is called "Superman," and it's written and performed by a band (not a person) named Lazlo Bane. It's a personal favorite.

All God's Chillun Need a Livin' Wage

(*Owed* to Our Economy)

If there was ever a time for the church to start preaching all the messages the Bible gives about money, wealth, and poverty, surely that time is now. I offer this piece of overwhelming evidence: times are so tough these days that even White House press secretary Tony Snow (who left his job in September 2007, just seven months before his untimely death from cancer in April 2008) gave "financial reasons" as his primary motivation for resignation. Mr. Snow's deputy press secretary, Dana Perino, succeeded him.

ABC News reported around that time that the press secretary earns $168,000 per year. I don't know if Mrs. Snow worked outside the home for a little extra income. The Snows have kids, so maybe she is a full-time homemaker. We all know that missing work (for illness or any other family crisis), combined with the exponentially rising costs of medical care, will set anyone back a good bit monetarily. And, obviously, the nature of his work for the White House prohibited him from working nights delivering pizzas for a little extra dough (no pun intended—well, okay, pun intended).

While many of us are fortunate enough not to know the stress that came with Mr. Snow's cancer diagnosis, we *can* empathize with a family's financial stress. I'm just a small-town Baptist pastor, and I know a lot of other preachers—from other towns big and small, and from other denominations. And I can tell you that we all wonder how our families are going to make it another two years; heck, many of us don't even know how we'll make it till the end of the month.

But then again, we all pastor some folks who don't know how they'll make it *till the end of the week.*

Many of my Christian brothers and sisters loved watching Tony Snow on Fox News, and many of my Christian brothers and sisters helped put his boss in office, who then gave him (and Ms. Perino after him) his low-paying job. Maybe Dana Perino or the next White House press secretary will remember the rest of us who are suffering, too. Perhaps they can use their connections with the bigwig politicians and business leaders to lobby for a living wage for every American citizen; use their connections to lobby for a dramatic overhaul of our health-care system so we can all receive the care we need; and speak up for all of us Christians who put politicians in office because they tout biblical values, but then do *nothing* to carry forth the biblical mandates for economic justice for all.

So rest in peace, Tony, and may God bless you and the family you sought to support. And may we all remember that you needed a livin' wage, I need a livin' wage, and all God's chillun need a livin' wage.

Note

[1] All quotes and references are taken from an article on ABCNews.com titled "Financial Pressures Force Snow Departure" by AP White House Correspondent Terrence Hunt, http://abcnews.go.com/Politics/wireStory?id=3493708, 17 August 2007.

Keeping Our Hands to Ourselves

(*Owed* to Mike Yaconelli)

"Why can't preachers keep their hands off their parishioners?!"

Mike Yaconelli, the late-great-pastor-for-people-who-don't-like-church, asked this question of William Willimon, the great-not-yet-late-bishop-for-people-who-do-like-church. Willimon was about to go out onto a big stage and speak to a large gathering. He was standing quietly, focusing his thoughts, reviewing his key points. And, just as the renowned Methodist minister was about to walk out to give his thoughtful speech, the non-ordained pastor and prankster grabbed Willimon's arm and asked the aforementioned question.

Willimon, now shaken up and his thoughts distracted, began walking out to the podium, and again Yaconelli asked—this time yelling it out loudly—"*Why can't preachers keep their hands off their parishioners?!*"[1]

Yaconelli never was one to let people feel safe and comfortable. He was, in many respects, a thorn in the side of the organized church for the better part of his life. Whether founding *The Wittenburg Door* magazine more than thirty years ago, or freelance speaking and writing in the years leading up to his death in 2003, Yaconelli loved Christ and Christ's church so much it hurt. And that deep love usually annoyed us inside the church a good bit, too.

Which is why Yaconelli's question won't go away: Why can't preachers keep their hands off their parishioners?

EthicsDaily.com keeps posting news articles about this topic and its silent history in Baptist church life. This cannot come as a surprise to any of us who have been associated with the church for any length of time.

A pastor quietly resigns and moves to another ministry position in another state. Did the Lord call him to another place of service? Actually, it's because the pastor "called on" a few other men's wives in the congregation.

A young woman turns her back on the church and deeply distrusts ministers. Why? Once, when she was a college student, a male minister to students dropped in for a friendly visit. She soon discovered that his idea of ministering to her as a student was more about meeting his lustful desires than her spiritual needs.

A beloved, well-respected, "successful" pastor leaves behind a trail of broken young men in numerous churches. Why? The pastor secretly enjoyed "teaching" budding teenage boys "the ways of manhood."

These are just three examples. Each one is true in its facts, but each is also true thousands of times over across the country, with a few minor variations in the details.

"Why can't preachers keep their hands off their parishioners?!" Yaconelli's question haunts all of us in our church buildings. But, as more and more well-kept secrets are uncovered, others are beginning to ask the same question.

As you search for an answer, take time and read some of Yaconelli's articles.[2] You'll hear Yaconelli wailing against the corporate success models of "doing" church; against the emphasis on a minister who can "bring" results, who can oversee numerical growth. You'll hear Yaconelli contrasting all of these "wonderful" things against the witness of our Scriptures, against the testimonies of Jesus and the disciples, and against the very nature of slow, messy, disciple-making soul work.

But don't just take it from me. Here is classic Yaconelli, from a piece titled "Run for Your Soul!":

The church has baptized busyness and activity and basically formed a pact with the devil. This pact has succeeded in silencing those who criticize the trend toward hectic, overworked, burned-out, spiritually dry ministers who—in the "name of God"—neglect their families, their souls, and their physical well-being.

A ministerial colleague once asked me if it is really important for a minister to care for her own soul. The minister, he reminded me, is paid to do the assigned tasks of teaching, preaching, administrating, etc., and to do them well. After all, people can't "see" a minister doing real, personal soul work. My heart sank. I'm almost certain I heard Yaconelli screaming from the heavens.

Maybe there is something about ministers neglecting their own souls—sometimes even being *expected* to sacrifice their souls—for the sake of other people's religious thrills. The result? Families, individuals, churches, and ministers suffer through abuse, manipulation, and tragic story after tragic story.

I know ministers, of course, who manage to keep their hands to themselves, but they also seem to fight tooth and nail to ignore the "rat race" of corporate church busyness in order to make time for "non-busy" personal soul-tending.

Just why can't preachers keep their hands off their parishioners? I don't know if Will Willimon ever answered Yaconelli, but I suspect Yaconelli was well on his way to answering the question himself.

And methinks he was onto something . . . .

Notes

[1] Will Willimon told me this once when I met him way back when, and he confirmed it again via an e-mail. That's about all the documentation I have; you'll just have to trust me, or you can ask the good Dr. Willimon yourself.

[2] Educate yourself—search the Internet for "Mike Yaconelli" and see what you can learn. Thanks, God, for Mike Yaconelli.

Confronting the Whore Within: A Lenten Meditation

(*Owed* to The Possum)

According to the church calendar, I am writing this during the season of Lent (which for me, as a New Orleans native, means we're somewhere between Mardi Gras and Easter). As a lifelong Baptist, that means I'm new at this party and still learning my way around in such things as "the church calendar." One thing of which I'm fairly confident is that Lent is a season for personal reflection, confession, repentance, and prayer.

If that is true, then poet/singer Derek Webb clearly expresses the meaning of Lent in his song "Wedding Dress."[1] The entire song is perfect for Lent, and it is captured in this pivotal line: "I am a whore, I do confess." That's right—Lent is essentially about acknowledging the whore within.

That's what Jeremiah tells us, isn't it?[2] The Prophet likes to compare God's people to a bunch of wild whores looking for lovers behind every nook and cranny; and, other than a lot of technological and bureaucratic advances in our abilities to be unfaithful, not much has changed since Jeremiah's time. We *still* run after little gods here and little gods there who promise us immediate satisfaction, immediate comfort, immediate productivity and prosperity, immediate power, immediate attention.

Yet, God *still* takes us back time and time again, only for us to turn right around later the same night, climb out the window with *another* little lover god, and do it all over again, and then again, and yet again. We just can't help ourselves: we will be seduced by marketing, business, politics, whatever: "I'll make you more successful, wealthier, and more powerful, if you just give yourself to me; I'll show you *paradise by the dashboard light!*"

The Prophet wonders, When in the world is God simply going to give up on His creation? *When in the world is God simply going to give up and stop loving us?* He complains and yells out at God; he wishes God would just leave *him* well enough alone; and he wishes that God would forget the rest of us—let us unfaithful cheaters go our own *damned*[3] way.

No wonder Jeremiah is so sad and depressed. It's like listening to George Jones (affectionately known as "the Possum") cry out that heart-wrenching story of a cheating wife who leaves her faithful and loving husband . . . that husband who lovingly and longingly waits for her to come home again. Until that one day when he finally stops loving her:

> You know, she came to see him one last time,
> and we were all wonderin' if she would.
> And it kept runnin' through my mind,
>   "this time he's over her for good."
> He stopped loving her today,
> they placed a wreath upon his door.
> And soon they'll carry him away.
>   He stopped loving her today.[4]

Yep. Jeremiah says *we* are that cheating wife! But, and he seems mad at God for having to say it, Jeremiah also promises us that God is *always* waiting and ready to welcome us back home again, because God is good, and His love *endures forever!*

The Prophet fights with this truth tooth and nail, but reluctantly acknowledges that, unlike the rejected husband in the Possum's song—*whose love only ends when he finally dies*—the eternal God is beyond death, and so God's great and patient love for us never ends.

God never stopped loving us yesterday. God doesn't stop loving us today. God will not stop loving us tomorrow.

Even when, in all of His love for us, He comes in the person of Jesus Christ and lives among us; even when we doubt Him, ridicule Him, abandon Him, and betray Him; even when we reject Him and crucify Him; even when we carry Him away and bury Him, and even when we place that wreath upon His stone . . . *even then* all our countless rejections and habitual affairs cannot keep Him from loving us, any more than they could keep Him in the tomb.

Yes, we are *still* jumping into bed with every god promising us whatever the "big thing" is at the moment. But, as Jeremiah grits his teeth in resistance from having to tell us this truth, God, whose love endures forever, will welcome all of us cheating, hell-bound whores back to Him as we sing His praises.

So with thanks to the Possum and the Prophet for the promise of hope in the faithful, loving God, let us spend this season of Lent reflecting and admitting with our hearts and our mouths the honest truth as worded by Derek Webb: "I am a whore, I must confess."

And thanks be to God that He *never* stops loving us.

Notes

[1] From Webb's album, *She Must and Shall Go Free*, INO Records, 2003.

[2] You can read the book of Jeremiah—which is longer than the book you are holding in your hands—later. Jeremiah isn't a nice, affirming book for an afternoon read.

[3] That's in the biblical, not expletive, sense—or perhaps it is in *both*.

[4] Oh yes! This is George Jones's 1980 country music masterpiece, "He Stopped Loving Her Today" (written by Bobby Braddock and Curly Putnam).

For the Love of God

(From a Cousin of Frank and Jesse James)

If Johnny Cash or Kris Kristofferson has ever portrayed you or any of your family members in a movie, raise your hand. My hand's up; how about yours?

My maternal grandfather's paternal grandmother—that's my momma's daddy's grandma on his daddy's side—was Margaret James from Missouri. According to family history, Margaret James, my great-great-grandmother, was a cousin to Frank and Jesse James. That makes me Frank and Jesse's cousin four times removed, which brings me back to Cash and Kristofferson. In the movie *The Last Days of Frank and Jesse James,* Johnny Cash plays my cousin Frank, and Kris Kristofferson plays my cousin Jesse.[1]

Some consider my James cousins Confederate folk heroes, the Robin Hoods of our nation. Some consider my James cousins nothing more than daring robbers and cold-blooded murderers. Nevertheless, my kinship ought to amount to something, don't you think?

Honestly, I'd like to get some V.I.P. treatment from this. But alas, I'm just another Joe Schmoe. Everywhere I go, I get the same treatment as you.

The truth is, we all like special treatment, don't we? We think we *deserve* special treatment.

Sometimes, it's because of our family heritage: She's a Hilton. They are Mannings. He's Britney's ex. *I'm a cousin, four times removed, of Frank and Jesse James.*

Sometimes it's because of something we do: The president decides things. The Donald owns things. Some guy named Barry writes songs that make the whole world sing things. *I tell people I'm related to notorious outlaws.*

Sometimes, it even invades the church: She's our Sunday school perfect attender. They've read all the "how-to-be-a-holier-than-thou-Christian" bestsellers. He speaks in tongues (or, for you Baptists, he has his own "private prayer language"). *I'm a cousin of Frank and Jesse James, and their daddy was a Baptist preacher.*

This sense of entitlement is nothing new; it plagued God's people from the beginning. The prophets point it out to the Israelites. Jesus exposes it among the religious leaders. And Paul unmasks it in young churches.

Here's the catch: all of this stuff is about *us*. It's always about us—*you* or *me*. And really, none of this stuff matters at all. Nope, it's not about our family heritage. It's not about what we do. And, I'm committing heresy here, but it's not even about how righteous we think we can be.

The truth is, it's all about God. It's about being in the presence of God, who is love; it's about letting God strip away all of these things about us and letting God form in us the likeness of Love. It's about letting God (Love) create an incarnate image of Love in you and me.

Larry Norman adapted the Apostle Paul's "love" theme for his early-1970s song "Righteous Rocker."[2] With some altering for today, Paul, through Larry—with a little help from this outlaws' cousin—might have this to say to us today:

> You can boycott Hollywood, and never go to Dollywood
> You can be as pure as you can be
> Or you can curse like a sailor, or write like Norman Mailer
> and experience everything you can see
> You can be friends with Albert Mohler,
> or you can dance like a holy roller
> But without love, you ain't nothin', without love
> Without love, you ain't nothin', without love
>
> You can be on a spiritual search, or you can live at your church,

You could have the most heavenly aims,
You could be an Adolph Rupp, or drink from a golden cup
You can be kin to Jesse James
you can learn to pray like Jabez prays,
you can find your purpose in forty days
But without love, you ain't nothin', without love
Without love, you ain't nothin', without love.

They say that though fueled by pride, anger, hatred, and greed, even cousins Frank and Jesse showed some glimpses of love—occasionally. I guess, then, that though the church often is fueled by pride, anger, hatred, and greed, maybe the world will even catch some glimpses of love—occasional glimpses of *Love*—through us.

For the Love of God, let's hope so.

Notes

[1] Maybe one day Willie Nelson will want to play *me* in a movie based on this book.

[2] You can check out Larry's original version on one of the greatest single rock and roll albums about faith ever recorded: the classic *Only Visiting This Planet*. You can get it on CD from www.LarryNorman.com. By the way, Larry Norman passed away during the writing of the book. Thanks, God, for Larry.

Beating Golf Clubs Into Guitar Stands

(Ode to the Allman Brothers Band)

I don't like golf.[1]

Many of my friends live to golf. One went so far as to compose an ode to the spirituality of playing golf. Meeting God on the golf course! I just don't get it.

The whole concept of golf is completely beyond me. If it doesn't involve trying to hit the ball into an alligator's mouth or under the dinosaur's foot, I don't see any fun in it. I prefer to listen to live music. I long for that great day when we beat golf clubs into guitar stands and turn golf courses into music festival sites.

Yes, I can't stand golf, but I love the Allman Brothers Band. *Now* we're talking about spiritual experiences! Yeah, that's right—I have spiritual experiences with God at Allman Brothers concerts.

Whereas some folks speak of the tranquility and the quietness of eighteen holes of golf, and others talk of the quiet stillness of meditating alone in a solitary place, I am alive with God in the middle of a crowd uniting under the soulful power of God's gift of music.

The joyous notes of "Statesboro Blues" and "One Way Out" fill me with charismatic joy. The lengthy jams of "Whipping Post" and "Jessica" take me on spiritual journeys. I close my eyes and the music carries me into God's Presence. During these musical excursions, God speaks to my soul; God's presence reaches out and holds me; God takes my hand and leads me places.

Don't even try to tell me otherwise. I've doubted it and questioned it myself. After all, I'm not in a church building; I'm not listening to a preacher, and I'm not even listening to an evangelically "authorized and approved" Christian rock band. There's nothing specifically "holy" in our mindset about a music festival, and certainly not an Allman Brothers show. Most of the folks present wouldn't set foot in a church, and if they did they'd be made to feel so uncomfortable and out of place they'd have to leave.

But hey, there's nothing specifically holy and moral about golf, either. Haven't you watched *Caddyshack*?[2]

God's creation, though fallen and sinful, is a holy creation. And music is a wonderful, holy gift from God. And, since God gives gifts and blesses whomever God wishes, I'm affirming that the Allman Brothers Band has been blessed with the holy gift of music.

Now, for all I know, Gregg Allman is a rabid golfer. If so, more power to him. I hope he lets his long blond hair down so it blows freely and that he wears a short-sleeved Harley Davidson t-shirt that exposes his multi-colored tattooed arms. Heck, if Mr. Allman invited me to hit a few rounds of golf, I'd bite my tongue and be off in an instant! Just as soon as I put on my tie-dyed blues-fest t-shirt and my cut-off jeans, and put in my earring . . . .

Notes

[1] Just in case you didn't get that, I **HATE** golf.

[2] For the record, I love *Caddyshack*—thanks be to God for the gift of Rodney Dangerfield.

Strain Out the Gnats! The Poo Poo Has Hit the Fan!

(Ode to Swallowing Camels)

It made big news not too long ago that President George W. Bush said "[the 's-word']." President Bush isn't the first Christian, nor the first president, to use a "naughty" word. Christian voters were appalled when White House tapes revealed Richard Nixon's fluent use of profanity. Christian/rock star/activist Bono even said the "f-word" on a nationally televised awards show.

Words, of course, can wield great power; and yet words only contain the power we give them. Words are but jots of ink on a page or syllabic sounds rolling from our lips. It's the *meaning* we give to words and how we *use* them that grant them such power.

One of my heroes, the great Harry Potter, dares to speak the name of his nemesis, Lord Voldemort. Other wizards fearfully refuse to say the name; instead, they emphatically whisper, "He-Who-Must-Not-Be-Named." Ironically, their fear of saying "Voldemort" gives the name great power over them.

It's like saying "the 's-word'" instead of just outright saying "[the 's-word']." We avoid four letters arranged in a certain order: not "t-h-i-s," nor "h-i-t-s," but an "s," followed by an "h," then an "i," and finally, a "t."

Of course, we talk about it all the time; we just use "nice" words and phrases like "oh, crap," "horse manure," or "clean up the dog poop." Imagine, if Mr. Bush had just said "poop," his comment to Prime Minister Blair would not even have made the news.

Sociologist and preacher Tony Campolo has told audiences that while they were sleeping the night before, some 30,000 children died of hunger, and that most in the audience "don't give a ['s-word']." Campolo then points out that more of them are shocked that he said a "bad" word than that children are dying of hunger. Campolo's point? Jesus emphasizes actions over words.

Repeatedly in his confrontations with religious leaders who are great at saying the "right" things, Jesus accuses them of *not doing* God's will. "Not everyone who says to me, 'Lord, Lord,' will enter the kingdom of heaven, but only the one who *does the will of my Father in heaven.*"[1]

My wife and I have a close friend who, according to a local newspaper article about her, "is not very fond of foul language." This came as a surprise to her and to us, as she once sat in our living room boldly declaring her intense fondness for "foul language." Four-letter words aside, she is a passionate follower of Jesus, a pastor's wife, and a fine preacher in her own right. Yes, she curses like a sailor, *and* her life radiates God's unconditional love to any and all people whom she meets.

Most of us, though, sit in our pews saying the "right" things and applauding leaders who say the "right" things. We are shocked whenever we hear certain arrangements of four simple letters.

All the while, we exclude people because they're not "good enough." All the while, the hungry grow ever hungrier; health-care costs prohibit more and more people from even the most basic services; our cities are filled with violence; and our nation is warmongering. But at least we know our words are "nice" enough for God.

Maybe we are the "blind guides" Jesus challenges when he says, "You strain out a gnat but swallow a camel!"[2]

Maybe, just maybe, Jesus doesn't give a ['s-word'] about what we say as much as what we do.

Notes

[1] The text is Matthew 7:21; the emphasis is mine.

[2] Jesus says this in Matthew 23:24.

A Psalm for Sherman

(*Owed* to Hunter S. Thompson)

Sometimes God seems so far away—or not present anywhere at all. It seems that whenever I feel this way, I always get behind a car with a bumper sticker that asks, "If you don't feel close to God, guess who moved?" It's as if God has set up residence in one place in time—and you can head toward God or move away from God. It's kind of like God is resting comfortably in Jerusalem, or, say, Mississippi, and you can drive closer to God or drive farther from God.

My friend Sherman[1] and I were discussing this once, and pondering the unbelievable improbability of God's ubiquitousness as described in Psalm 139. That's the psalm that states no matter where you run, no matter where you hide, no matter where you go, you cannot escape God's loving Presence; that even when you make your bed with death itself, God is there.

In other words, God is not sitting still in one physical location waiting on you to come to Him. God is everywhere—*everywhere!*—all the time, waiting for you.

Then Sherman stunned me. "God spoke to me once in the pages of *Playboy*," he said.

Now, come on, Sherman. Hugh Hefner's publication of naked girls for men's lustful eyes? Really. But Sherman explained: One day he wasn't in the mood to be holy—truthfully, he was annoyed with God about more than a few things—and he went out and bought an issue of the men's "entertainment" magazine. In the midst of being "entertained," he noticed one of the articles—it was an interview with the now-deceased gonzo journalist Hunter S. Thompson.

Sherman began reading the article. Somewhere in the interview, which in typical Hunter S. Thompson form was saturated with obscenities and wild, exaggerated stories, Thompson began discussing the Bible. Sherman says he was impressed with the depth of Thompson's biblical knowledge. But when Thompson quoted Proverbs 26:11, Sherman dropped the magazine and cried.

Proverbs 26:11 says, "Like a dog that returns to its vomit is a fool who reverts to his folly."

"Right there," said Sherman, "in the middle of an interview with a drug-loving, foul-mouthed, hallucinating journalist, and between pages of naked women, God spoke to me."

Sherman the fool had deliberately "turned his back" on God and ran to his folly. Yet, even in the midst of wallowing in his own "vomit," Sherman learned that there really is no place he could go where God is not. Apparently, not even in an exploitative porno magazine.

Because of Sherman, I now believe—even though it still blows my mind—in the unbelievable improbability of God's ubiquitousness.

Note

[1] Of course this isn't his real name, and like "Deep Throat" of Watergate fame, I will protect his identity until he decides to reveal it himself.

Sweeney Todd: Vengeful Barber of Biblical Proportions

(Ode to Tim Burton)

I recently saw *Sweeney Todd: the Demon Barber of Fleet Street*.[1] If you've seen this musical, then you know: it is disturbing yet beautiful, haunting and tragic yet brilliant. Yes, there's blood. Lots of blood. And then, even more blood. It is, after all, a musical about a serial-killing, throat-slashing, revenge-obsessed madman (and that's not even getting into the deceit that turns Londoners into unknowing cannibals).

So it's obvious, isn't it? When it comes to making biblical movies, forget Cecil B. DeMille! Tim Burton is the only choice for director. Think . . . *Beetlejuice. Edward Scissorhands. The Nightmare Before Christmas. The Corpse Bride.* Burton is a visual genius, with a subtle touch for heartfelt stories of the tragically human. Remember, our Old Testament is overflowing with tragically human stories involving sex, rape, murder, merciless vengeance, and, of course, celebratory songs about all of it.

Consider *Sweeney Todd.* A barber named Benjamin Barker is falsely imprisoned simply so that a lustful judge can have his way with Barker's wife. I hear echoes of David the king and Uriah the Hittite (see 2 Samuel 11). Unlike the lustfully murderous King David, however, the lustful judge in our musical only *imprisons* the barber for fifteen years. Barker returns a cynical and bitter man, and then is informed that his wife committed suicide. The obsessed barber changes his name to Sweeney Todd, and he mercilessly seeks revenge upon the judge (and many, many others!). It's throat-slashing, blood-spewing gore, with singing, dancing, and music. It's like watching Norman Bates star in *Oklahoma!*[2]

Burton handles the tragedy and the beauty of it all so masterfully. It could have become so trite, so typical—a bizarre attempt to marry Broadway with gross-out teenage slasher flicks. But, in the hands of Tim Burton . . . *wow.*

Now then, who else can tell the tragic stories of the Bible (talk about sex, violence, rape, murder, and vengeance!) without either whitewashing it to make it unrealistically super "holy" or making it some cheap sacrilegious orgy of violence worthy only of midnight showings and small cult-like followings?

It's the book of Judges, though, in which I think Burton's talents could really shine. Think about it: An old man welcomes strangers (a Levite, his concubine, his servant, and some donkeys) into his house for the night, feeds them, gives them a place to rest, cares for the animals, etc. Sexual perverts show up at the old man's door later demanding to have their way with the Levite; the old man, thankfully, stands up to the mob. Instead, the old man graciously offers the mob—sort of as a consolation gift, I guess—his own virgin daughter and the Levite's concubine. They refuse, demanding the Levite himself. The Levite tosses his concubine out the door to the mob, and they rape her repeatedly all night long. The Levite opens the door on his way out the next morning and yells at the abused concubine, collapsed on the ground, "Get up and let's go!" The story ends with the Levite cutting her into twelve pieces and sending a piece of her to each of the twelve tribes of Israel (see Judges 19).[3]

If that's not enough, there are musicals, too! There is Deborah (the prophet and judge), Barak (a military man), and a woman named Jael. Jael lures Sisera (Barak's and Deborah's enemy) into her tent under the guise of hiding him for his safety; she gives him some milk, and he falls asleep on her floor. Once he's asleep, Jael grabs a hammer and a tent peg and—wham! talk about spewing blood!—she drives that tent peg into his temple, through his head, and right into the ground. And then, you guessed, it, Deborah and Barak burst into song:

> He asked for water and she gave him milk,
> > she brought him curds in a lordly bowl.
> She put her hand to the tent-peg
> > and her right hand to the workmen's mallet;
> she struck Sisera a blow,
> > she crushed his head,
> > she shattered and pierced his temple.

It is a long song full of praises to God mixed with details of gruesome violence, and it even mocks Sisera's mother waiting in vain for Sisera to return home. The song ends with a plea for God to let all of God's enemies die as Sisera did, while God's friends shine like the sun (you can read the whole gory tale in Judges 4 and 5).

Yes, Burton is the right man—the only man—for the job. The Bible is filled with tragic stories of evil people and good people who do terribly evil things (and sing songs, too!). Burton is the only one who has proved he can capture the grotesqueness of our humanity as a heartfelt tragedy. And essentially, that's what the Bible is, isn't it? A truly disgusting story of human sin—over and over and over again—and God's never-ending love and pursuit of us in spite of ourselves. And nobody can capture that essence on film better than Tim Burton.

Imagine Johnny Depp as King David and Helena Bonham Carter as Bathsheba. I can't wait!

Notes

[1] Warning: This is not a movie for the squeamish, nor is it child-friendly. So, after the kiddos are asleep, pop some popcorn and enjoy!

[2] This may have made *Oklahoma!* more interesting to me. Don't get me wrong, I love Shirley Jones—Mrs. Partridge herself once kissed me on the cheek at a Mardi Gras parade. But letting Norman Bates star in *Oklahoma!* would have probably kept my attention. After all, everything's up to date at the Bates Motel.

[3] Feel free to read it for yourself in Judges 19. It's not the best night-time-about-to-go-to-bed devotional material.

Gays, Baptists, and Killer Tomatoes

(Ode to Bible "Experts")

My friend Michael[1] and I have a lot in common. We were both born and raised as Southern Baptists in the Deep South. We both applaud the brilliant absurdity of the film *Attack of the Killer Tomatoes*. And we're both gay. Well, most of the time. I'm often frustrated, sad, or just flat tired. But when I'm not one of those things, I tend to be gay. Michael, no matter how he's feeling, is always gay.

I was confused, then, when I heard that a prominent Southern Baptist Seminary president may or may not have suggested that babies might be born gay, and if they are, we Christians may or may not have the responsibility to tinker about in the womb to ensure that they will *not* be gay.[2]

Why would any Christian not want another person to be gay? If we're receiving the full and abundant life Christ offers us, I'd think we'd all be gay and enthusiastic from time to time.

My wife says I'm missing the point. Apparently, the word "gay" has another meaning besides happy and excited. So I looked it up in Webster's. There are the usual definitions such as "happily excited," "keenly alive and exuberant: having or inducing high spirits," and "bright, lively."

But then, sure enough, there is a fourth: "Homosexual; of, relating to, or used by homosexuals."

My wife went on to explain that is why I am sometimes gay and sometimes not, but why Michael simply *is* gay. "Same word, different meanings," she said.

Oh.

So, thanks to my wife, I now understand that Dr. Albert Mohler, president of the Southern Baptist Theological Seminary, is not so much saying that genes that cause exuberance should be altered in fetuses, but rather genes that may lead to homosexual behavior.[2]

I'm still confused, though. Here's why: I've known Michael and his family since I was a kid. He has been and still is an active leader and teacher in church. Yep. Michael's gay (by the fourth definition), and yet I still know him to be a man of deep and sincere faith. And because I know Michael, I cannot imagine going back in time to alter his genetic makeup in order to make him some sort of super-über-Christian. Hey—I've watched *Frankenstein* enough to be scared to death of trying to play God with creation.

Dr. Mohler argues in defense of his prenatal care plans for gay fetuses with ten points for consideration.[3] Though well thought out and clearly stated, I find it odd that Jesus is never mentioned in these important points that "Christians who are committed to think in genuinely Christian terms" should ponder.

Maybe I'm not as "committed to think in genuinely Christian terms" as I had hoped, but I don't understand why Dr. Mohler fails to refer to Jesus. I went to the Gospels to find out and—lo and behold!—Jesus has absolutely nothing to say about homosexuality. N-O-T-H-I-N-G.

Jesus does, however, have an awful lot to say about high-and-mighty religious experts speaking on behalf of God about who is "good" enough and who is not quite or nowhere near "good" enough for God. God's self-appointed "spokesmen" in the Gospels[4] are the very ones who, in protecting their religious power and traditions, despise Jesus and lead the charge to crucify him.

According to the Gospel accounts, Jesus has no time for petty religious games, and he prefers love over law and grace over judgment (though he sure comes down hard on the religious experts!). One of the preeminent teachings of Baptists is that Jesus is the ultimate revelation of God to humanity; therefore, all of Scripture is to be interpreted through the life, death, resurrection, and teachings of our Lord. This, then, leads me to believe that Jesus is more likely to be hanging out with Michael and his friends than sitting around in a comfortable room of Bible experts discussing the top ten proper "Christian" ways to think.

The next time I watch *Attack of the Killer Tomatoes* in my gay enthusiasm (by the first few definitions), I'll think of my gay friend Michael (by the fourth definition) and wonder if he is sharing a laugh with Jesus as they watch one of our favorite movies together.

Notes

[1] Only my friend's name has been changed to protect the innocent.

[2] "Is Your Baby Gay? What If You Could Know? What If You Could Do Something About It?," blog post by R. Albert Mohler Jr., www.AlbertMohler.com, Friday, March 2, 2007.

[3] Not ten commandments, mind you, but ten genuinely Christian assertions he makes in his article.

[4] Yes, spokes*men*. These "God experts" in the Gospels are always men.

Prostitution, Politics, and Grace in the Big Easy

(*Owed* to a House in New Orleans)

A pornographer, a prostitute, and a public official walk into a . . . Wait. Sorry. This is no joke. It's actually the sad content of a news story I just read. While perusing the Internet for news about the LSU Tigers and looking for some signs of hope for my New Orleans Saints, another article caught my wandering eye.[1]

The report is about the U.S. Senator David Vitter, who represents Louisiana, the state of my birth. It is also about Wendy Yow Ellis, a prostitute in New Orleans (the city of my birth), and Larry Flynt, the notorious sleaze peddler (with whom I have no birth connection). Here's what I gather from the article:

- Sen. Vitter campaigned and got elected on a platform of morals and family values;
- the senator allegedly also had ongoing "business dealings" with Ms. Ellis in a French Quarter apartment;
- Mr. Flynt is obsessed with the senator's "business dealings" with Ms. Ellis;
- Ms. Ellis is now making *really* good money telling her story to Mr. Flynt, and letting Mr. Flynt show the world what she showed the senator in the privacy of that French Quarter apartment; and, finally,
- the Tulane Green Wave will likely *not* be the C-USA football champions this year (wait, sorry, that was a different report).

The senator insists he has never "done business" with the prostitute in question, though after his name appeared in the phone directory of the "DC Madam," the senator acknowledged a "very serious sin" in his past. Now, if we'd let him do his job, the senator wants to get on with his business of protecting the sanctity of marriage from the gay menace.

Something about this article keeps hounding me. Maybe it's because I dearly love the city where I was born and raised. Maybe it's because I love reading about the slime that is Louisiana politics. Or maybe it's because I can't stop singing "The House of the Rising Sun." "There is a house in New Orleans they call the Rising Sun, and it's been the ruin of many a poor boy . . . ."

If Mr. Flynt can produce some serious evidence connecting Sen. Vitter with Ms. Ellis (and Flynt seems convinced he's got what he needs), this may well become the senator's theme song. As a man who is sick of politicians using God and the Bible to get elected, I want to cheer the exposure of such hypocrisy on the part of the powerful (recognizing, of course, that hypocrites reside in both parties).

As a pastor who tends to cheer for the underdog, I'm glad to see Ms. Ellis get her story out there, and I'm even okay that she's getting paid a hunk of money from Larry Flynt to do it. Maybe now she'll have the money she needs to live a better life and can stop selling her body. Her story reminds me of one of Faulkner's tragic, sorrow-filled, almost-doomed-but-essentially-good characters. I hurt for Ms. Ellis.

But as a follower of Jesus, I can't get rid of some nagging sense that I should also be hurting for Sen. Vitter and even Mr. Flynt. I don't want to.

I know the Bible has a lot to say about the powerful, the wealthy, and about those who exploit others for their own gain. Yes, the Bible has a lot of harsh things to say about men like the senator and the pornographer finally reaping what they've been sowing. Their time is gonna come, all right.

Yet, something about Jesus keeps pricking my hard conscience. Something about Jesus keeps jabbing at me to see Vitter and Flynt as broken men. Something about Jesus keeps nagging me to stop judging them.

Or maybe it's something about the Blind Boys of Alabama singing "Amazing Grace" to the tune of "House of the Rising Sun" (which is playing over and over on my iTunes), that has me mixing grace with prostitution.[1]

Sure, it makes me sick that both men have used and abused women so flippantly for their own pleasure and gain; sure, it makes me sick that both use their money and power to be movers and shakers, to manipulate and fight; and sure, I abhor their politics and their sense of values (or lack thereof).

But, doggone that nagging Jesus, I think I'm going to pray for them too. I think I'm going to pray that when they come to terms with their own brokenness, if and when they do, that maybe in the midst of all the people jumping up to kick them when they're down, someone will be there to reach out a with hand of mercy and grace to the hurting men. And by the grace of God, may I be in the latter category rather than the former.

Now if you will, let's all stand and sing, in your deepest, bluesiest, howling-est voice, and to the tune of the classic folk song about a brothel,

Amazing grace! How sweet the sound!
That saved a wretch like me!
I once was lost, but now I'm found!
Was blind, but now I see!

Notes

[1] Kate Moran, "Prostitute, Flynt Keep Pressure on Vitter," Nola.com, 17 September 2007, http://blog.nola.com/updates/2007/09/prostitute_flynt_keep_pressure.html.

[2] You can check out this version of "Amazing Grace" at http://www.youtube.com/watch?v=iDSZrB0vEKQ.

Ain't Nobody Here But Us Chickens

(Ode to Poultry in Motion)

I don't know nuthin' 'bout raisin' no chickens. I'm a city boy. I've lived and worked in or near a big city all my life so far, and I can count on one hand everything I know about chickens: (1) I love the old Louis Jordan song, "Ain't Nobody Here But Us Chickens"; (2)Popeyes chicken is spicier than KFC chicken; and (3) the best way to get someone to do what you want them to do is taunt them and call them "chicken."

I know even less about hens: (1) the number one fear of married men is that their friends will think they're "henpecked"[1] and (2), well, that's really about all I know.

Oh, and Jesus says something about wanting to act like a mother hen gathering her brood under her wings (see Luke 13:34).

Now, I don't know nuthin' 'bout no chickens and no hens, but I know about Karla and her son. My friend Karla and her husband were both raised in the church, are committed followers of Jesus, and raised their son in the faith and in the church. As the son entered his late teens, he began going his own way. By his senior year and into his early college years, the son explored many of life's options outside of the faith of his parents. Some of his choices were risky, dangerous, and had potentially harmful long-term consequences. How Karla longed, longed so deeply it hurt, to embrace her son and hold him safely in her arms. And how Karla's heart broke time and time again as her son continued going his own way.

The theme of Luke 13:34 is a familiar theme throughout the Scriptures. God's people, the Hebrew people, the Israelites—they never behave. In fact, they are so proud of being tagged as "God's chosen people" that they won't even listen to God; not only will they not listen, they even attack and kill the messengers God sends them.

Rebellion. Rejection. God's children. Karla's son. You and me. All of us revolt against our heritage and explore our own paths to some degree or another.

The overriding image, though, is of God's broken heart for wayward children. God in Christ Jesus longs, longs so deeply it hurts, to embrace the children of Abraham again, to hold them safely in his arms. And God's heart breaks time and time again as the children continue going their own way.

We are familiar with the Loving Father image of God—especially as Jesus calls God "Abba" (a personal, affectionate term like "Daddy"), and as Jesus describes a father's longing for a child to return home in the story we call "The Prodigal Son."

Here, though, Jesus presents another image to say the same thing. Jesus—God incarnate/God in flesh and blood—describes his love for *us* as that of a mother hen. A mother hen trying to round up, to gather up her beloved chicks under her wings, to keep them close, for warmth, for comfort, for protection. But the chicks revolt and continue wandering away from the mother hen's secure and loving wings.

Luke 13:34 gives us a powerful image of a rebellious people, and it gives us a glimpse into the broken, longing heart of God in Christ Jesus.

No, I don't know nuthin' 'bout raisin' no chickens. But here is an image of God's love for all of us—an image of a mother hen brooding . . . an image of a mother hen trying to gather up all her chicks under her wings.

So here we are . . . and there ain't nobody here but us chickens. And, thank God, a persistent Mother Hen.

Note

[1] That's the number one fear of *most* married men . . . sorry, honey!

The James Brown 3-Step to an Active Faith

(Ode to . . . well, James Brown)

How does God move us from inactive faith to active faith? Someone asked me this question, assuming that since I'm a seminary-trained *professional* Christian,[1] I'd know more about faith than other folks. I replied that you can spend any amount of money at any Christian bookstore on any number of "how-to" manuals guaranteed to deepen your faith, strengthen your faith, or even make you more active in your faith. And, if that works for you, more power to you, my friend.

I, on the other hand, have no such prescription. I'm certainly not one to be giving advice. I can only speak of my own experience; and, as for me, God has been using a lot of James Brown. Yes, sir, the God of All Creation has been using a whole lotta Godfather of Soul to move me from inactive to active faith recently.

It primarily involves three songs (er . . . *steps*).

(1) "Get Up Offa That Thing"
I've discovered that anytime I'm not feeling well (physically, emotionally, soul-fully), "Get Up Offa That Thing" makes me get up and move like nothing else.
Get up offa that thing, dance till you feel better!
Get up offa that thing, and shake till you feel better!

Believe me, it works. I'm up and about . . . washing dishes, exercising, or browsing through books on my shelf. And I'm up and

shaking, dancing, moving around the room. James Brown is right—
shaking and dancing sure do make you feel great! I also discover I'm
no longer self-absorbed in my inactivity, but absorbed in the
Presence of God all around me. I'm listening for God, and I'm looking for God. I'm ready to act toward others as God wants me to act
toward them. I'm even ready to start acting toward myself as God
wants me to act toward myself. Like King David, I can get so caught
up in the presence of our loving God that I dance until the cows
come home, though as of this time, I have been able to refrain from
dancing around in the streets in nothing but my unmentionables.[2]

(2) "Get Up, Get Into It, and Get Involved"
Faith is action. Faith is being and doing and doing and being. Even
when you don't believe anymore, as Daniel Bailey says, "faith is
believing when you don't believe." So just get up, get going, and get
involved. Go out there and pray. Go out there and do justice. Go
out there and love mercy. Go out there and walk humbly with God.
Get moving. Just do it. No matter how badly I'd rather rot on my
couch than face the world again, I'm always better off when, by
God's grace, I can somehow manage to get up, get into it, and get
involved.

(3) "Say It Loud (I'm Black and I'm Proud!)"
Yes, that's right, I'm a spoiled middle-class white boy from the sub-
urbs, but who doesn't feel better when this song comes on? Nothing
overtly spiritual here, except that anything that moves me from inactive to active faith has to be a good thing, and this song moves
me—it gets me up offa my thing, it reminds me that God is not a
white middle-class Protestant American male, and it gets me
involved. Besides, I dance, and that *always* makes me feel better.

   Will this work for you? I don't know, but it can't hurt. I suggest
trying the James Brown method of moving from inactive to active
faith:[3] First, get up offa that thing; second, get up, get into it, and
get involved; and third, and say it loud (I'm black and I'm proud!).

And by the grace of our Lord Jesus Christ and the power of the Holy Spirit, may the James Brown trilogy of soulful inspiration move you from inactive to active faith.

In the interest of full disclosure, this three-step method was first developed for a larger Bible study on a passage from Second Chronicles (go figure!) written for the Green Lake Conference Center, Green Lake, Wisconsin.

Notes

[1] Whatever *that* means!

[2] If you are not familiar with David's infamous underwear dance before the Lord, see 2 Samuel 6:14-15.

[3] Just three simple and easy steps to a healthier, happier, more active faith!

Confessions of an LSU Convert

(With Apologies to Mother)

My mother met my father about forty-five years ago in New Orleans. Cast aside all those images of French Quarter debauchery! Mom met Dad when they were both students at Tulane University, at a college Baptist Training Union gathering at the historic St. Charles Avenue Baptist Church. After courtship and marriage came a young family.[1]

My sister and I were raised to love God as good Baptists, and as good Tulane Green Wave fans we were raised to hate all things related to the Louisiana State University Tigers.

I must confess, though, that I have strayed from what Mom and Dad taught me. I have a weakness, a serious moral flaw: I *love* winning. For most of my life I was able to lose gracefully (and even learn how to *have fun* while losing) by being a Tulane Green Wave fan. In the state of Louisiana, Tulane sports were always number two. We were the minority.

Although Mom and Dad never taught me to believe that Baptists could—and *would*—save the world, I came to believe it. My need to win found its hope and its outlet in Baptist dominance. We would win the culture wars, the "my-denomination-is-more-right-than-your-denomination" wars, the "God-loves-*us*-more-than-God-loves-*you*" wars, and so on. Yes, my need to win and my need to be an obnoxious, arrogant, rabid winner channeled itself into my personal faith and support of the Baptist church. Yep, we Baptists were indeed number one!

Then in 1986, right after my high school graduation, Mom and Dad moved the four of us to Jackson, Tennessee. I have lived several places since then—Kentucky, Mississippi, and Memphis, Tennessee, but I've never again resided in the state of my birth.

Over the past twenty or so years away from Louisiana, I've discovered that Tulane makes few "waves" in the national world of collegiate sports, except baseball. On the other hand, no matter where I've lived, I can't help but hear about LSU—in *all* sports. Yes, in the world of Louisiana sports, even as it's covered around the country, LSU is undeniably number one.

The longer I've been away from the Bayou state, and the more I miss the Bayou state, the more I've enjoyed hearing about the Bayou Bengals of LSU. As the years have passed, the hatred I harbored toward LSU has faded. In its place a swelling of pride has grown: pride for the people of my home state, pride for the team of my home state, and pride for the national attention paid to my home state. After all, most of my neighbors and friends in school were LSU fans. Some of them even attended LSU. One of my best friends, Marta, went on to play her flute and piccolo in the LSU band.[2]

Today I proudly stand with them and, with obnoxious and rabid enthusiasm, chant L-S-U! L-S-U! L-S-U!

The funny thing is, as my prideful and arrogant fervor for the LSU Tigers has grown, my dependence upon the church to be a dominant force has waned. In fact, I have grown to see that the church's job is *not* to dominate, *not* to win and boast, but *to serve*, quietly and humbly, as Jesus himself *served* quietly and humbly. The purpose of the church is not to be number one, or even number two, fifteen, or twenty-five. The purpose of the church is to be *last*—even willing to *die!* We are to be the *salt*, not the main course. We are to be a *candle*, or a *light bulb*, not the sun itself. We function best as a minority, *not* the ruling majority. Our victory is in Christ, after all, in God, and not in our buildings, our baptisms, our budgets, and in no way in our cultural dominance.

So, you see, as God has refocused my views of faith and the church to be more Christ-centered, and as God has taught me that Micah 6:8 is not just a sweet little verse but *a way to live*, my ability to be last and to lose gracefully has transferred itself from Tulane sports to the church. Now my personal need for greatness and dominance, removed from the important places of faith and church, resides in a less important place—college sports.

Mom, guess what? Cheering for LSU is actually a spiritual discipline! It channels that nasty need out of the church and away from faith, where it does terrible damage, and into a fun activity like big-time collegiate sports. Yep, it's a little easier to be focused on loving justice, doing mercy, and walking humbly with God when I can use LSU as an outlet for pride, arrogance, and dominance.

And, Mom, since I'm writing this on your birthday, I must say, "I love you! Happy birthday, Mom!"

And, since I'm writing this just prior to the college football national championship game in January 2008, I *must* yell, "Geaux Tigers!"

Notes

[1] Out of two children, I'm number two. This fact may be of importance.

[2] For the record, I went on to play my trombone in the Mississippi State University Maroon Band, and this confession of an LSU convert only means that LSU has moved up to second place behind my first love, the Mississippi State Bulldogs.

A Tale of a Man-Date

(*Owed* to Arlo Guthrie)

It started out just like any other man-date: I won two tickets to see Arlo Guthrie in Lexington, Kentucky. My wife was unable to go with me, so I invited my good friend Daniel Bailey. We met up at Mellow Mushroom Pizza, had a pre-concert dinner that couldn't be beat, and talked about Jesus and his mandate—you know, to care for the poor, the neglected, "least of these." Then, we made our way on over to the performance hall to be serenaded by the legendary folkie.

It was a great concert filled with great songs and great stories about great things like peace and love and, of course, shovels and rakes and implements of destruction. The first song Arlo sang was his 1973 classic "Last Train"; it was as if Arlo himself had been listening in on our conversation at the Mellow Mushroom and decided to sing this first song just for Daniel and me:

> Maybe you've been lying down in the jailhouse
> Maybe you've been hungry and poor
> Maybe your ticket on the last train to glory
> Is the stranger who's been sleeping on your floor.

After the concert, at midnight, Daniel and I stood between our two cars and were saying goodbye when out of nowhere a third person began walking toward us—and by out of nowhere I mean that where there was nothing but the two of us, our two cars, and an empty parking lot, there appeared a man just a few feet away walking toward us. He told us he was homeless. He told us he was an addict. He told us he was on his way to a long-term residential rehab facility in a nearby city. He told us he needed a place to stay for the night.

So here we were talking about Jesus' mandate to care about the poor and the outcasts, singing Arlo songs about community and love, and ready to go back to our comfortable homes and climb into our comfortable beds, and then here comes this homeless guy asking us to do unto him as *Jesus* would do unto him. I mean, if we take Jesus *seriously*, if we really take Jesus at his word . . . here comes Jesus—Jesus! In the person of a young homeless man! Jesus! Coming to two ministers of the gospel of Jesus Christ as if to see if we were going to let our lives bear witness to what we'd been talking and singing about.

And with great hesitation on our part, with no game plan to guide us, and with nobody to help us if this situation turned violent, together Daniel and I took this homeless man who wanted us to treat him as Jesus would have treated him to a nearby motel. We got him a room, bought him some food, gave him some cash, said a prayer for him, and said goodnight.

Daniel and I got back into my car wondering if we did the right thing, wondering if the homeless man would even stay in the room that night, get some sleep, get up the next morning and enjoy a breakfast at the Waffle House next door, then get on a bus and go to Cincinnati—which is what he told us he was going to do. We wondered if he was going to take the little bit of cash we left him and leave the room and blow the money on alcohol or drugs or to get into the strip club a few blocks away. We drove back to the still-empty parking lot asking ourselves all these questions, second-guessing ourselves, and trying to convince each other we weren't complete idiots.

I'm not so sure anymore that Jesus lets us see the results of our actions—whether they are wonderful, give-thanks-to-God-we-helped-someone results, or if they are boy-we-got-duped-and-manipulated-and-enabled-an-addict-to-hustle-another-day results. Jesus in the Gospels doesn't seem to care as much about what *other people do* with our generosity as about whether or not *we* are loving and generous and kind and merciful and forgiving.

Jesus doesn't tell us he's going to hold us accountable for what other people do with what we give them. Jesus only tells us he's going to hold us accountable for whether or not we freely give.

Which brings me back to Arlo. Remember Arlo? This is an ode (actually, an *owed*) to Arlo. Maybe an old hippie folksinger understands Jesus better than this seminary-trained-paid-professional clergyman (and most others I know).

Maybe your ticket on the last train to glory,
is the stranger who's been sleeping on your floor.

The Ballad of John and . . . John

(Ode to John Lennon)

Every year when December hits, we hear a lot about John. That's John, as in the strange and hairy man screaming as loud as he can that we've really messed up the world, and we had all better get our act straight before it's too late.

I was twelve years old when John was killed. I can still remember hearing it on the news, that 8th of December in 1980. My favorite radio station, WRNO-FM,[1] played nothing but John Lennon or the Beatles for what seemed like an entire day or more. Every year since then, early in December, John's life, death, and message get told again and again.

The same is true of another John. Another strange and hairy John screaming as loud as he can that we've really messed up the world, and we'd all better get our act straight before it's too late.

Early in the Christmas season, as the church observes Advent, this other John's life and message (but not so much his death) get told again and again. Pay attention in your Advent worship services, and you may hear a lot about this other John.

This latter John we call "the Baptizer"; the former one we call "the Beatle." In addition to their name, appearance, and message, they share other characteristics, too. Like the prophets Elijah, Jeremiah, and Ezekiel before them, both Johns stood out from the crowd with their personal grooming habits. They both were also fond of using bizarre, dramatic public behavior to draw attention to their message.

John the Baptizer was jailed for speaking out on the immoral personal behavior of the powerful and corrupt ruler, Herod Antipas. Herod, out of fear of the people, resisted his urge to kill the Baptizer, until a young woman[2] danced the hootchy kootchy so well that a drunken Herod surrendered to his wife's wishes and had the trouble-maker's head cut off.

John the Beatle was spied on by the FBI for speaking out on the immoral and corrupt behavior of the powerful United States govern-ment. President Nixon fought fiercely to have the Beatle deported, but lost the battle. In the end, it was not the government but a deranged fan who eventually killed this troublemaker.

There are also some important differences. The Baptizer lived and died *during* Jesus' earthly life; the Beatle, almost two millennia *after* Jesus' earthly life.

The Baptizer, after being thrown in jail and not seeing any signs of a Messiah-led power play, dared to question Jesus' identity as the Christ. The Beatle, after being mocked, ridiculed, and targeted by Christians and the U.S. government, dared to call upon Jesus' iden-tity as the Christ.

Remember the Beatles' 1969 hit, "The Ballad of John and Yoko"? Each verse tells of the rejection and mocking John the Beatle faced for his beliefs and strange actions, and in the chorus John cries out, "Christ, you know it ain't easy, you know how hard it can be, / the way things are going, they're gonna crucify me."

One John dared to question Jesus' identity, yet we praise him as a prophet and a saint. The other John identified with Jesus' suffering and hardships, yet we demonize him as sinner and a heretic.

Perhaps the Beatle was intentionally taunting Christians; per-haps he sincerely felt persecuted by "God's people" in much the same way Jesus was persecuted by "God's people." Or, perhaps . . . *both.*

But when compared to our powerful, selfish, and self-preserving "Christian" lifestyles, the Beatle seems to have had a far greater understanding of and appreciation for Jesus' life, death, and teach-ings than those of us boasting about our Christianity. Take for example Jesus' words about suffering, persecution, and taking up one's cross.

Yes, we hear a lot about two Johns every time December rolls around. One tells us (as reported by Eugene Peterson), "What counts is your life. Is it green and blossoming? Because if it's deadwood, it goes on the fire." The other is telling us (as reported by John and Yoko), "Give peace a chance," and "War is over (if you want it)."

I think God may be using both Johns to try to tell us something. Maybe, just maybe, we *all* need to do some repenting . . . and imagining.

Amen, and goo goo ga joob.

Notes

1 As in "We're the Rock of New Orleans!" I don't know if, after all these many years, it is still a great rock-and-roll station or not.

2 Herod's stepdaughter, by the way.

When Love Comes to Town

(A Christmas Meditation)

December 2007

> In the beginning was the Word,
>> and the Word was with God,
>> and the Word was God . . . .
>> And the Word became flesh and lived among us.
> (John 1:1-2, 14a)

Or, as Eugene Peterson puts it, "The Word became flesh and blood, and moved into the neighborhood" (*The Message*).

Fourteen years ago this Christmas day, my son Rob was born. Fourteen years ago, *life* presented itself to my wife and me in all of its messy and glorious wonder. Christmas will always be a time for Jency and me to remember that *life* has come.

Christmas is a time to celebrate life. You will be together with your mothers, fathers, sisters, brothers, spouse, children . . . and you will be filled with joy and wonder at all the life that surrounds you. You will be reminded that *life* has come.

Twenty-two years ago this Christmas day, on a one-lane, pine-covered Mississippi back road, my cousin Jeff died in a car wreck. At twenty-three, Jeff was my oldest cousin, and I admired him deeply. Twenty-two years ago, *death* presented itself to me in all of its ugliness and unfairness, in all of its deep sorrow and pain.

One Christmas, *life* came to Jency and me in the form of our firstborn child. Another Christmas, *death* came to my Aunt Myra and Uncle Butch and took away their firstborn child.

Christmas always reminds us that *death* has come. This Christmas you will be without a mother, father, sister, brother, spouse, child . . . and you will be confronted with the grief, sorrow, pain and confusion that remain with you when *death* has come.

Two thousand years ago our Lord and Savior, Jesus Christ, was born. Christmas always reminds us that God Himself has come to us in the form of a little baby.

I once heard a musician, Michael Bridges of Lost and Found, say, "God spoke a word of Love, whose name was Jesus." Using a bit of liberty with Scripture, and keeping this wonderful thought in our mind—God spoke a *word* of *Love*, whose name was *Jesus*—listen again to John's Gospel:

> In the beginning was *Love*,
> > and *Love* was with God,
> > and *Love* was God.
> > *Love* was in the beginning with God.
> > And *Love* became flesh and lived among us . . . .

Or . . . *Love* became flesh and blood, and moved into the neighborhood.

And here we have the wonder-full, awe-filled, mysterious beauty of Christmas: Here with us where *life* has come in all of its messiness and glorious wonder, and here with us where *death* has come with all of its ugliness and pain, *Love* has taken human form and *moved into the neighborhood!* And when *Love* comes to town, all sorts of strange, remarkable, and unbelievable things begin to happen.

> When *Love* comes to town
> > every valley is filled in
> > every mountain and hill are made low
> > the crooked roads are made straight
> > the rough ways are made smooth
> > and humanity sees the salvation of God. (Luke 3:5-6)

When *Love* comes to town
    good news is preached to the poor
    freedom is proclaimed to the prisoners
    sight is recovered for the blind
    release is granted to the oppressed
    and the year of the Lord's favor is proclaimed. (Luke 4:18-19)

When *Love* comes to town
    the wonder of *life* is increased;
    the joy of *life* is magnified to its fullest;
    and the awe and mystery of *life* blossom forth at every turn.

When *Love* comes to town
    the ugliness and pain of *death* are eased;
    the sting of *death* is taken away;
    the power and finality of *death* cease to be.

And when *Love* comes to town
    the deeply dug chasm between the created and the Creator is
filled in;
    and God reconciles women and men to God's self.

Another musician, Bono, puts it this way in the U2/BB King song "When Love Comes to Town":

I was there when they crucified my Lord
I held the scabbard when the soldier drew his sword
I threw the dice when they pierced his side
But I've seen Love conquer the great divide![1]

Yes, we still live with the glory and the messiness of *life* in our neighborhood; yes, we still live with the grief and unfairness of *death* in our neighborhood; but at Christmas, we are reminded that all is not just *life* and *death*.

In the midst of the *life* and *death* that will be with you this Christmas day, hear the good news: *Love* has come to town and moved into *your* neighborhood!

Note

[1] "When Love Comes to Town," by U2 and B. B. King. Originally released on *Rattle and Hum*, Island Records, 1988.

Part 2

Sanity Means Admitting You're Completely Nuts

*May we never forget the words of the late-great prophet
Waylon Jennings: "I've always been crazy,
but it's kept me from going insane!"*

The Disney Totem

(Or, Why I'm a Baptist Preacher)

Will Campbell tells of a friend named Thad Garner. Thad was somewhat of a rough-talking, arm-twisting, manipulative type of man from Louisiana who knew how to get things done. But more importantly, Thad Garner was a Baptist preacher. One day while having a frustrating hunting experience, the Rev. Garner tore into a storm of vulgarities, prompting Will to ask, "Thad, why did you ever decide to be a Baptist preacher?" Thad, somewhat upset by the question, declared, "'Cause I was *called*, you (expletive) fool!"

Offensive? Of course! But there's something terrifyingly true here. When the shock (or, hilarity!) of the cussing preacher wears off, I am faced with this offense: each of us has specific gifts for specific purposes over which we have no control. Our choice is simply whether or not to heed the call.

"'Cause I was *called*!" Thad said.

Not long ago some old friends treated my family and me to a Disney movie. *Brother Bear* is an animated feature about a Native American growing from a boy into a man. He is given his totem: a small statue representing a particular virtue he will come to embody. He rejects this particular totem—it is not consistent with his self-identity; it is not what he envisions for himself. We follow him on his journey through which he is constantly at odds with this totem. Certainly, he was given the wrong totem; surely, the totem-giver was mistaken. But through great struggles, some of them life-threatening, he becomes aware of and accepts *who he is*, and he indeed comes to personify his totem. There simply is no escaping it.

"'Cause I was *called*!"

Brother Bear treated me to an epiphany in, of all places, the cinema bathroom. While washing my hands, I looked into the mirror.

There stood the young boy who somehow *knew* that he would be a preacher; there stood the boy hearing extended family talk about him being "the preacher in the family" (which came first: the "knowing" or the "hearing"?). There stood the rebellious heavy-metal preteen. There stood the church-loving teenager active in his youth group. There stood the token hippie at the small Baptist college and the long-haired, ear-pierced rabble-rouser failing at his first try at seminary. There stood the radical sociologist ready to change the world and the depressed cynic who had given up on the world and on life itself. There stood the man of renewed faith rocking and rolling with youth groups and the apostate who denounced his belief in the program-oriented life of the church. There *I* stood.

As I type, Willie Nelson and Waylon Jennings are singing through my computer speakers. Compact discs, vinyl records, and cassette tapes surround me. I look up and see an Elvis clock, his legs swinging back and forth as the pendulum. My walls are covered with posters of the Beatles, Bob Dylan, and the original Woodstock Music Festival.

But just as visible in this hippie-hillbilly-counter-cultural shrine are Bibles, commentaries, and books galore about God, the church, and humanity. Favorite quotes from Shakers and Quakers, monks and preachers are plentiful. Hymns and church music are also frequently heard. And, taped on the wall next to Elvis's time-keeping hips is a photo of me with Will D. Campbell.

Other than being from Louisiana, I don't have much in common with Will's friend, Rev. Thad Garner. But come visit me sometime and let me tell you about meeting B. B. King or interviewing Arlo Guthrie. Come spend a day with me at an outdoor music festival and you'll soon learn that if I had my druthers, I'd rather talk with Neil Young than with just about any "important" religious leader you could name.

You see, then, why I am confused as to why I'm an ordained preacher. Yet, here I am. It's for reasons too mysterious for my own understanding and for reasons I have no right to know.

It's 'cause I've been *called*!

Will *Not* Work for Grace

Grace.

It was God's grace that literally saved me from my own self-destruction ten years ago. God's grace that gave me life again; that gave me my family again and that gave *me* back to my family; that gave me meaning and purpose again; and that set my feet on this path that brought me to Baptist Seminary of Kentucky and placed me in the pastorate. Yet, in spite of all of this overwhelming presence of grace at work in my life, I still struggle with and resist God's "little" graces every day (of course, they aren't "little" at all).

I owe Dr. Glenn Hinson a final exam *and* a research paper for Church History from last year. I took incompletes in all three of my courses, and completed two of them by the end of the spring semester. I was well on my way to making good progress on researching the answers to the final exam, as well as clarifying the working hypothesis of my research paper, in addition to keeping up with the first few weeks of readings for a new course I just started, when the news hit of my impending surgery. Then the amount of recovery time set me back further.

I essentially lost almost two months of my life—family, church, and seminary. Now, once again, I'm trying to dig myself out of a big hole at seminary. I already arranged to take another incomplete in this new class due to the surgery.

Yesterday I met with my academic adviser to discuss my spring schedule. I intended not to take any classes, except an independent study I can do from home. This would free me to complete the Church History work and the other course, and to be back on my feet and out of the hole by the end of spring semester.

I explained to my adviser about my "incomplete" in Church History from a year ago—which now has a "B" officially registered on my transcript. He urged me to talk with the esteemed and legendary Dr. Hinson about this—does that "B" free me from the debts of missing assignments and allow me to take the "B" and move on, or do I need to complete the required work? I was uncomfortable doing this. I want to keep my promises to Dr. Hinson and to myself. I don't want to get "something for nothing." Nevertheless, my adviser instructed me to ask Dr. Hinson and to state upfront that my adviser told me to ask—the answer determines what I do in the spring.

I had supper with Dr. Hinson last night before classes to discuss our possible meeting with Will Campbell. I put off bringing up the subject of Church History at first, but finally I had to ask.

Dr. Hinson said that he knows I am capable of doing good work. He knows I attended classes all the way to the end and that I still had my books and class notes as future resources. If I'm happy with a "B," then I should take it. He would have expected me to get an "A," though.

Tears welled up in my eyes. I don't deserve this. It's not fair to other students, nor really to me. Then I remembered: I actually *did* complete Church History under Dr. Glenn Hinson—in fall 1990 at the Southern Baptist Theological Seminary! I got a "C"—because I didn't study at all. I was too busy organizing protests on campus against the first Bush's intentions to go to war with Iraq. I remembered that and mentioned it to Glenn. I told him I did a research paper on Meister Eckhart, and I described the doctoral student who was the grader for the class. However, I hadn't wanted the "C" transferred in because I wanted to take the course and study this time around; besides, the president of the Baptist Seminary of Kentucky, Dr. Greg Earwood, said he couldn't transfer in a "C" from another institution.

This eased my mind. I'm not *really* getting something for nothing! I did complete the course once; so this last fall just gave me opportunity to attend class, review the notes again, do a mid-term, and pull the grade up to a "B."

Wait! *I am struggling with and resisting God's "little" graces!* My professor and my adviser are pouring out grace upon me, and I cannot accept it! Why must I attempt to justify deserving it by my own works?

Buechner writes of grace, "There's nothing *you* have to do. There's nothing you *have* to do. There's nothing you have to *do*. . . . There's only one catch. Like any other gift, the gift of grace can be yours only if you'll reach out and take it. Maybe being able to reach out and take it is a gift too."[1]

I was offered a tremendous gift of grace, but I was unable to receive the gift by simply reaching out and taking it. I resisted to the very end, until I could finally justify for myself that I should take it.

God, forgive my stubborn and foolish, self-absorbed pride. Thank you for making me struggle with grace, and thank you all the more for the graces that come my way every day. Help me be able to receive only by your grace.

And thanks be to God for the Baptist Seminary of Kentucky, Dr. Glenn Hinson, and Dr. Rick Landon (my adviser). A seminary that teaches *and lives out* grace . . . what a concept!

Note

[1] See Frederick Buechner's thoughts on "Coincidence" found in *Wishful Thinking: A Seeker's ABC*. My creased and ear-marked copy is the 1993 revised and expanded HarperSanFrancisco edition.

I Dreamed I Saw Thomas Merton

I dreamed I saw Thomas Merton, alive as you or me. He was at a retreat with me—not the leader, but a fellow participant.

His presence was so calming, yet at the same time bursting forth with joy. I approached him during a break and introduced myself. His response to me and interest in me were as though *I* were the renowned author, and it was *his* pleasure and wish to talk *with me*.

I want to think that I shared with him my encounter with Jesus while eating lunch in silence at Gethsemane. I want to recall that we talked of that holy place and of prayer. But I can't be sure.

I do know that we shared together our fondness for Glenn Hinson, and he enjoyed listening to how Will Campbell has made me struggle fiercely with institutions. He shared his memories of Glenn and Will with me. I don't recall anything about those stories, just the wonderful feeling of listening to him as he shared them.

I awoke saddened that the visit had ended, but as calm and peaceful as I have ever awakened. I don't know what this dream means, other than, as Buechner says, it's a little whisper telling me I am in the right place at the right time.[1]

Thanks to Bob Dylan for the first line (taken from his song "I Dreamed I Saw St. Augustine"), and thanks be to God for Fr. Louis's[2] holy visit in the night.

Notes

[1] See Frederick Buechner, "Coincidence," in *Wishful Thinking: A Seeker's ABC* (rev., and exp., San Francisco: HarperSanFranisco, 1993).

[2] Thomas Merton's "monk name" (as he was known at the Abbey of Gethsemani)

A Chicken in Every Pot, Salvation in Every Soul

Once a friend asked me, "Who are you in the pulpit?" We talked about this for a little while, and the question haunted me the rest of the day.

One night in 2004, as I drove home from Lexington after a seminary class, I listened to the Republican National Convention on NPR. I heard a few speakers, including Senator John McCain. McCain was a good speaker. He said some powerful things—not that I agree with him, mind you, but he said them well and in an inviting manner. He got the folks excited and riled up, which at any political convention is an important task. But somewhere toward the end of his speech (by which time I was angrily shouting back at him in the privacy of my car), I realized that *this is what I do*!

Am I nothing more than a politician in God's name instead of some party's name? Am I just someone who tries to get folks excited about my particular theology?

All of us preachers—regardless of theological orientation—get behind our platforms and preach our agendas and hope to get the folks behind us. Same techniques, same skills. Politicians . . . preachers . . . public speakers all. What's the difference? Both John McCain and Bill Clinton could be great preachers behind pulpits.

Are we all the same? *Is that all I'm doing? Is* this *who I am in the pulpit?*

I began to think about Jeffrey coming to my house a week and a half after I preached a sermon that stuck with him and spoke to him. It was a message, Jeffrey said, that spoke of the deep mystery of God and spoke to the mysterious depths of himself.

Maybe I am not a spokesperson for some political party. Maybe I am not a pawn for any politician or a particular agenda. Maybe in my better moments I am an agent of God's eternal truth that reaches out through who I am in the pulpit (and in person) and touches a person in the congregation. In my better moments . . . and in spite of myself!

In my worst, though, I am a politician of sorts. I, too, have my agendas and pet causes and theological ideas I promote and try to get the people to support. Yet for some reason God *can* still move through all this mess to do what God wants to do in spite of me.

The Girl of My Dreams

One Sunday night a while back I didn't sleep well. I kept my wife awake for a couple of hours. She said she thought I was possessed or that something horrible and demonic was happening to me. She didn't know what to do. She said I was mumbling loudly, but speaking unintelligible words as if speaking in tongues or some unknown language; that I was breathing funny, my body was jerking around, and I was kicking.

Here's what I know: I was dreaming. I dreamed that the doorbell rang and there on our front porch, in the middle of the night, was a young, abandoned girl. We—my family and I—took her in and eventually began the process of adopting her.

As she grew older, she started having violent outbursts—cursing and flailing her body about as if *she* were possessed. Much of my dream involved Jency and me struggling to hold her legs and arms down while we calmly spoke to her, spoke her name, and told her we loved her. It was an intense and exhausting dream.

Jency told me she was scared to death by how *I* was acting while I was asleep—while I was dreaming. Was my body responding to my dream by trying to hold down this girl, or was my body acting out the part of the girl? Jency tried to demonstrate my speech to me—and said it went on for *two* hours. She said she even went to the bathroom during all of this and heard me mumbling and moving in my sleep from the bathroom!

The next night, after she told me this and we talked about my dream, Jency and I watched our weekly episode of *The X-Files*. It was about Fox Mulder and *his* dreams of finding young murdered girls.

This made me think a lot about Mulder and a lot about me. I love *The X-Files*, and I consider Fox Mulder to be one of my personal heroes (Dana Sculley is an added bonus). Fox isn't afraid to listen to his emotions and his intuitions. Fox will not be a "company man" (or in this case a complete FBI agent). He is true to himself; true to his search for the truth; and true to his longing to believe that there is more going on around us than what we can see and know and definitely more than what we are being told.

I understand that. I want to be more like Fox Mulder. I don't like being a company man. I want to be able to be true to myself, to my faith, to my God—regardless of the consequences from the group/organization/institution within which I am employed. Yet here I am struggling with a congregation that employs me over things like the meaning of worship and what and why we do things in our worship services (do we do them to please *us*?).

I'm tired. I'm frustrated. I can't say what I want to say because I'm employed to be *their* minister. I'm not a prophet. So, do I serve God as I best understand God, or do I serve a group of people?

I keep thinking about becoming a writer and a freelance speaker/preacher so that I can set my own schedule and freely say what I think needs to be said. I'm tired of being responsible for everyone else and every little thing that goes on in a church. And here I am again with my existential angst . . . worried about tomorrow and not living in today.

This brings me back to my own dream. What does it mean? I've given it a lot of thought, and I have two possible meanings.

In one meaning, the church is the little girl that came to me out of the blue and whom my family took in. As a pastor I am trying to love her, to help her mature, and to give her a safe and secure holy setting in which to do so; but she doesn't understand such love. Instead, she erupts in outbursts of frustration and anger. I'm wearing myself out trying to calm her down and assure her that we love her.

There is, though, another possible meaning. In it, *I* am the little girl and the church is the family that took *me* in. *I'm* the one unable to handle where they are and what they do. *I'm* the one kicking and screaming and disrupting their lives.

Who knows? Maybe it means I should have eaten a better supper.

Either way, I disturbed Jency all night, and I woke up with a splitting headache and an upset stomach. I slept most of the day and missed my Monday night seminary class.

My body always has a way of stopping me when I get stressed and anxious and don't make time to rest. But looking ahead at more school papers and projects, church-related conferences, and constant petty bickering . . . well, my body had had enough.

Blessed *and* Depressed

One of the terrible lies we tell in the church is that "Christians" don't get the blues. Once you "have Jesus," everything will be all right. Once you "know Jesus," it's all happy-happy, joy-joy from here on out. The lie is best summarized in the bumper-sticker slogan, "I'm too blessed to be depressed!"

The truth is that the blues do visit Christians from time to time. For some of us, our melancholy does more than just visit—it unpacks and moves in! Yes, it is true: we may be blessed, but many of us still get depressed; and some Christians get *very* depressed.

Why are we surprised? After all, some of our biblical heroes had terrible spells of depression and despair: Moses, Jeremiah, John the Baptist, and maybe even the great Apostle Paul. And don't forget Elijah, the patron saint of depression!

Yes, even among people of faith, long periods of darkness can cloud the mind. Yes, even Christians will shut down and withdraw when depressed. The harder they may try to do simple and usually enjoyable tasks, the more impossible it becomes to do those tasks. They will withdraw from work, withdraw from friends, withdraw from family. Depression brings with it an incomprehensibly deep sense of isolation.

How do I know these things? Because I'm a person of faith, one who strives to follow the Way of Christ Jesus, and an ordained minister of the gospel of our Lord, and I frequently struggle with depression.

I can't provide anyone a "surefire" solution to depression, nor can I offer anyone "foolproof" methods of helping someone else "snap out of" depression. I can share that, in my own journey, depression has set in and led me into a spiritual crisis during a period when I was spiritually unhealthy. Depression has arisen during times of great change and transition (a move, the death of a friend or loved one, even the end of seminary semesters). Depression has come upon me at all sorts of times, in all sorts of circumstances, and even when I've been the most spiritually *healthy* that I have ever been.

What I have learned to do in my struggles with that thick, dark fog enveloping me is to share with my wife and my closest friends how I'm feeling. I need to know that others are watching out for me, because my vision gets too blurred to see clearly my thoughts and actions and what is going on around me. When the depression lingers for too long, when it disrupts my family and my work, I have also learned to seek counseling and medication.

I often escape into Harry Potter novels. I particularly get enthralled by Harry's attempts to fight off those frightening Dementors. I sometimes write down my thoughts, feelings, observations, and dreams.

Oh, and I pray. I pray the Psalms, especially Psalms 40 and 126. I pray; remember the past; try to hope for the future; and I pray desperately for God to act in the *now*.

"How long must I wait, God?"

"You've saved me before, God; *do it again!*"

Then I watch the winds blow by; I feel the earthquakes shake my foundations; I sweat as the fires consume everything around me; and I listen for that still, small whisper of hope from my Creator and my Redeemer.

And, even though I'm depressed, I try as hard as I can to look around at my family and friends and remember that I am also very blessed.

Remembering . . .

Lately, I've been remembering the last days of August 2005—when Hurricane Katrina hit the Gulf Coast. So many memories surfaced that week as I obsessively followed the news, checked internet web sites, and made hundreds and hundreds of attempts to contact friends and neighbors—all in vain. At the time, of course, I had no idea how they were, or where they were, or whether or not their houses were damaged or destroyed.

Remembering. Sometimes we call it just being nostalgic, a melancholy moment of escaping back into the past.

But it's not simply that, at least not most of the time. Remembering somehow calls up from deep within us that which we are, that which has shaped us and influenced us, and that which is still shaping and influencing us even now, though we may not even be aware of it.

Remembering short family trips to the Mississippi Gulf Coast—Biloxi and Gulfport and Mobile, Alabama—where we did touristy things and swam in the Gulf of Mexico.

Remembering going with my dad to Wand Rubber Stamp Works, Inc., the business in New Orleans on Magazine Street of which he was president and co-owner. He would take me with him some Saturday mornings, and I'd earn a little money sweeping stairs and cleaning windows. Then I'd go look for rats on the largely vacant third and fourth floors of this historic uptown building. Remembering that Kenny and Big Sal and Little Sal and Ms. Marie were not just people who worked with Dad, but that they are life-long family friends.

Remembering the schools I attended: Airline Park Elementary in Metairie; John Curtis Christian School in River Ridge; and Destrehan High School, in, of course, Destrehan.

Remembering my church: First Baptist Church of Norco (NORCO—New Orleans Refinery Company) and Bro. Jimmy Knox who baptized me there. Bud Granier and Pam Smith and Kirk Banquer—my Sunday school teachers.

Remembering high school—too many memories, if that's possible. Great teachers like Ms. Bourgeois and Mrs. Chaisson, and the band director, Mr. Charles Catalano. Teachers who took a great interest in their students, or at least in challenging *this* student.

Remembering my neighbors: the Graniers, the Vitranos, the Robicheauxs, and the Schexnaydres. Remembering friends at church and at school: Robbie Cambre, Trey Granier, Bill Caughman, Mary Madere, Marta Gieseler, Debbie Induni, and Ronny Chilton. I have maintained some level of regular, sometimes frequent, contact with only a few them since I moved away in 1986—and in the past few years even that has been far too sporadic.

Remembering playing trombone in the historic St. Louis Cathedral in the French Quarter, and marching numerous times inside the Louisiana Superdome—even at the halftime of a New Orleans Saints game.

And remembering only evacuating New Orleans one time for a hurricane. More often than not, we stayed put. I remember specifically a smaller hurricane when I was probably about seven or eight; I helped Dad put masking tape on all the windows to keep the glass from shattering, and then we sat close together inside the house. I clearly remember walking outside into my front yard during the eye of the hurricane—a dead calm . . . a most eerie feeling.

But this is *not* simply nostalgia. No.

Remembering all of this is summoning up inside of me the core of my being. This is *who I am.*

The New Orleans area and its people are an essential part of my very being—having shaped and influenced me directly for the first eighteen years of my life, and still shaping and influencing me today, though I may not always be aware of it.

Remembering . . .

Help! I'm Trapped in a "Fat Elvis" Stage, and I Can't Get Out!

Graduate school was often rough and stressful as I would finish up one semester, crash through a summer course, and then try to catch my breath before launching into the fall semester. Often during these frantic seasons, I—somewhat knowingly—resisted and ignored my spirituality and my faith.

One night during such a time, I was preparing to "teach" and "lead" the practice of *Lectio Divina* (praying the Scriptures) at church. The text was Ephesians 6. It's the one about struggling with rulers and authorities and powers of darkness, and putting on the whole armor of God. I had read it a few times, in two or three translations, when *The Message* got me. "Pray long and hard," it says. Pray long and hard! How about praying at all? That'd be a start.

I guess I had been struggling with rulers and powers of darkness in my own life, and had been doing it by my own strength—no armor of God, and very little prayer. And I was losing quickly. Depression, bitterness, distraction, gluttony . . . the "shadow" sides of my personality began having a field day.

I had become grossly overweight. I couldn't even muster the energy to play ball with my boys. I started just "getting by" at church and at school—by the seat of my pants, and not in a "good" way. In my good times, I can coast a bit and it's okay; a gift even. But not like this.

I always joke with people who get past the age of forty-two, telling them they've outlived Elvis, which is pretty good in my book. The way I was living, I wouldn't even outlive Elvis—and I'm *not* doping it up. But I *was* eating myself to death.

Something my friend Jim said to me has echoed in my head ever since. He works with hospice in Louisville. We talked of the meaning of "palliative care." In contrast to much of modern science and medicine (which seeks to fix and cure everything), palliative care helps treat the symptoms and the pain in order to help the person live as high a quality of life as possible—even though the illness remains.

I have been thinking about this for a while. Dreaming of Memphis will not cure church frustrations. Prozac and Strattera are not my cure for depression and ADD. I'm just past forty, and I'm on high blood pressure medicine, but they aren't my cure for high blood pressure. These are good things, yes—but they are to help lessen the pain and the restrictions of the symptoms. I must take the active steps to live more healthily, freely, joyfully, faithfully. The quality of the rest of my life is up to me—not the meds.

Funny—another twist: I have been working on an article for Smyth & Helwys's *Caleb's Cafe* online community. One of the key verses shaping the article is Proverbs 26:11, "Like a dog that returns to its own vomit is the fool who returns to his folly."

I have been the fool! And my folly has been my laziness, rebelliousness, and gluttony.

Not long ago, I could have died after a short stint of yard work; I had heat exhaustion and I was dehydrated. After this scary episode, I noted my thoughts, feelings, and frustrations about my health in an email to Michael:

Michael,
Have you ever noticed that "hell" is an essential sound when saying "health"?
Anyway, with my depression and high anxiety from a few months back—which led to terrible overeating and binging on

junk food and Dr. Peppers, and a total lack of physical exertion . . . all that combined with a high level of stress at the end of the semester and through the summer, I have high blood pressure—I mean like consistently in the 140s and 150s over 100s range.

Last Thursday afternoon I mowed our yard (which as you know is not a big yard), went to a short nominating committee meeting (already not feeling well), then came home and basically collapsed on our couch. I started throwing up. My head was killing me. My heart was racing. I was dizzy. Jency looked up heat stroke on the internet, but came across heat exhaustion and dehydration.

My body was HOT. Jency sent the boys to the IGA to buy Gatorade. She got several handtowels and a bedsheet wet with cold water and placed them all over me. I slowly sipped on Gatorade and finished off a bottle and a half in about an hour and a half—then got dizzy again (sitting down!), my head was hurting something awful, and I eventually threw all that Gatorade up (violently). My hands and feet went numb and tingly and I was having trouble breathing. By this time it was after 11:00 pm. The kids were in bed.

Jency wrote down some emergency numbers and placed them next to Rob and Daniel. She woke them to tell them to stay in bed; that she's taking me to the hospital in LaGrange. (I miss my little boys, but it's nice that they're a bit older at moments like this).

We arrived at the ER at almost midnight. They took me quickly, and pumped two bags of something into my veins. My head felt like it was going to explode, and my blood pressure had gone way up again, so they gave me a shot of something through the IV that would bring my blood pressure down and should ease my headache. Thirty minutes after that I was feeling better, and released. We got home at 4:00 Friday morning.

Had a few lightheaded moments throughout the weekend. Tuesday night we went to Wal Mart and bought a do-it-yourself at home blood pressure monitor. Went back to the doc today for a follow-up—still with steady blood pressure readings in the mid-140s over 100s.

He added another blood pressure medication (I'm now taking four different medications).

I'm dizzy and light-headed with a mild headache right now. Been drinking gallons of water for several days now. Eating more bland foods and some fruit and vegetables. Jency and the boys wanted to go to Cracker Barrel for lunch yesterday, so we went— and I ate my fries with NO SALT.

I'm not sure I can change my lifestyle. I'm not sure I can do it while barely keeping up with the church and trying to finish one more semester of school. I knew I was a health hazard—but I was hoping I could make it till December . . . finish seminary, start everything fresh and new.

I've got to get out of my fat-Elvis stage. It didn't work too well for him, and it isn't working very well for me.

Bert

And he replied like the pastor, mentor, and true friend that he is:

Bert,

Sorry about your recent unhealthy bout. Truly am. I'm sure it was scary for you, Jency, and the boys.

Now, for the other side of the coin. You and my dad have a lot in common when it comes to health and personal responsibility. Dad eats his salt and fries and sugar and carbs and lots of them. He doesn't use his C-Pap for sleep apnea. Life without salt, fries, sugar and with a C-Pap is not life, he says. High b/p, weight gain, lack of exercise is a time bomb waiting to happen. My dad is 75 and partially paralyzed. If he would rather die than make changes, I can accept that. You are young, with a lovely wife and two great kids. Two questions, particularly about the kids:

Do you want them to grow up with the same unhealthy habits their father has—and the same outcome? Do you want them to grow up without a father? Your choices have lasting impact on others. Your choices determine the impact.

As for making life-style choices later—after school, etc., there is no *later*. You either make changes in time or the time to make them never comes. There is no utopian time. We are always busy and dealing with stressors. . . .

Love you, man—really do and would like to have you healthy enough to tote my casket in about 43 years. A century is long enough for me.

Michael

Thanks, God, for Jency, and my sons, Rob and Daniel, and friends like Michael.

How to Flunk Hebrew Without Really Trying

"A funny thing happened on my way to seminary graduation: I had to take Hebrew." "Take biblical Hebrew . . . *please!*"

But enough with the one-liners. For many of us, well, for some of us, I mean at least for me, Hebrew was no laughing matter. I aimed high with my expectations in Hebrew (a solid passing grade—a "D" or, at best, a "C").

This doesn't mean I didn't want to learn. Oh, I learned a whole lot of stuff. I learned that the Hebrew word meaning "he built" is the word used when God creates woman in Genesis. So, the comment "she's really built!" may in fact be biblically sound. I also learned that given the choice between cramming for Hebrew and playing Scrabble with my family, I'm going to pick Scrabble just about every time.

Now don't get me wrong. I loved my seminary classes, and I respect my Hebrew professor, Dr. Greg Earwood. But the crux of the matter is this: At the time, *I was thirty-eight years old.* Jency and I had been married seventeen years and had two sons: Rob was almost thirteen; Daniel was ten.

When I walked into my first class at the Baptist Seminary of Kentucky, Rob was nine and Daniel six. For four years I'd had my nose in a book, my hands at a keyboard, or my body in a classroom. I couldn't shake the notion that I'd been missing my boys' childhoods. There were several consecutive days during semesters in which I hardly even talked to Jency, Rob, and Daniel, other than "goodbye," "hello," "I love you," and "I'll be up late typing, sleeping late, then leaving for seminary."

I added my own voice to Harry Chapin's classic, "Cat's in the Cradle": "When you coming home, Dad?" "I don't know when; but we'll get together then, Sons. You'll know we'll have a good time then!"

Oh, by the way, Harry Chapin was *thirty-eight years old* when he died in a car wreck, leaving behind his wife and children.

A biblical scene also haunted me. A woman breaks an alabaster jar and pours expensive perfume on Jesus' head. People complain (as would I) about the cost of the perfume and how many poor people could have been fed had the perfume been sold instead of wasted like this. But Jesus responds, "For you always have the poor with you, and you can show kindness to them whenever you wish; but you will not always have me" (Mark 14:3-9 NRSV).

I know it's terrible exegesis. I know it's taking liberties with Scripture. All I'm saying, though, is that I heard this repeated over and over again in my heart: "You will always have Hebrew with you, and you can study from your books any time you wish, but you will not always have your children or your family."

I think it was Tipper Gore, rock-and-roll-loving wife of Vice President Al Gore, who once famously led the chant, "It just doesn't matter! It just doesn't matter!" Or, maybe it was Tripper Harrison, Bill Murray's *Meatballs* character. Tipper . . . Tripper . . . an easy mistake we all make. Either way, it just doesn't matter. I've also heard the "it just doesn't matter" chant repeating over and over again in my heart.

In twenty years, nobody will care if I made an "A" or a "D" in Hebrew. They probably won't even notice the seminary diploma hanging on the wall. So, you see, *it just doesn't matter*!

In twenty years, however, Rob and Daniel will know what my priorities were when they were kids. Jency and I will know if we were good parents and loving partners to each other. So, you see, *Hebrew will always be around to learn and study . . . but my kids are kids and my family is a family for just a short time.*

Truthfully, I do respect Dr. Earwood's knowledge of biblical Hebrew, and I know I can go to him any time I am curious about it. Likewise, I hope he knows he can come to me any time he is curious about Harry Chapin or the movie *Meatballs.*

So, exactly how *do* you flunk Hebrew without really trying? I don't know, because I scraped by *without* flunking. But I do know that from now on, anytime Jency and I sing "she's a brick house" along with the Commodores, and Rob and Daniel shake their heads in disbelief and embarrassment, I will fondly remember Dr. Greg Earwood and my fellow classmates.

If I Ever Get Back to Memphis, I'm Gonna Nail My Feet to Beale Street

"I got my snakeskin britches, alligator shoes, money in my pocket, and a Memphis attitude," wails Gregg Allman in the Allman Brothers Band song "Midnight Man." Every time I hear it, I go nuts. Absolutely berserk.

Ahhh . . . Memphis. Beale Street, Elvis Presley Boulevard, Union Avenue, and Highway 61. The National Civil Rights Museum, the Peabody Hotel, and, of course, the mighty Mississippi River.

Elvis, Carl Perkins, and Johnny Cash. Rufus Thomas, B. B. King, and Booker T. and the MGs. And don't forget the Rev. Al Green!

Memphis is the home of the blues and the birthplace of rock and roll. It's chockfull of soul, and it's the home of my heart.

But alas, I now live in Henry County, Kentucky, northeast of Louisville toward Cincinnati, Ohio. With my Memphis attitude, my rock and roll sensibilities, and my love of cultural, religious, and ethnic diversity, I'm a bit of a stranger in a strange land way up here in the land of cattle, tobacco, basketball, horse racing, and Protestant domination.

Strangers in a strange land. It's a common theme throughout Scripture—Abraham, Joseph, and Moses. Shadrach, Meshach, and Abednego. The entire Israelite people from time to time.

God seems to enjoy sending people to strange and foreign lands in which they do not know or understand the local people and their customs. In such a situation, I guess, they are forced to rely upon God since they have nothing else. Sometimes I wish God wouldn't do such things.

I have no idea what these wonderful folks in rural Henry County, Kentucky, think of this big-city on-the-go rock and roll fan, but I'm pretty sure most of them like me. I've certainly been somewhat disoriented without stoplights, twenty-four-hour donut and waffle shops, music stores and performance halls, and locally owned pizza delivery joints.

Undoubtedly, folks here scratch their heads in bewilderment when they learn I used to have shoulder-length hair and wear an earring, and that I still would if I thought I could get away with it. And I scratch my head in bewilderment when I learn that many of these folks have never met a Muslim, never talked with people who went to school with Elvis, or never even had their cars stolen.

Yes, like many a Hebrew people in the great old Hebrew stories, I am a stranger in a strange land. And, like the Israelites of the Diaspora, I sometimes miss my homeland something awful. I occasionally drive into the Highlands area of Louisville and hang out at a local pizza joint that reminds me of my favorite pizza joint in Midtown Memphis—the Memphis Pizza Café. I go to this Louisville spot for the atmosphere: the wall murals and graffiti, the wide variety of music playing; the mixture of all kinds of ethnic groups; interracial couples; freaks, geeks, hippies, punks, whites, blacks, yuppies, dropouts, and professionals; and just about every other category you can think of. There I get a little taste of Memphis (plus really great pizza!) if only for an hour or so; and then I return to Henry County, where I live and serve.

I don't know why God takes people to strange and unusual places, but I know God has called me to be here at this time and in this place to serve Him and to serve those He places around me. I know God has not abandoned me; that God is caring for me, walking with me, guiding me, and providing for me. And, truthfully, I do enjoy and love the people in Henry County.

Yet in my most melancholy of moods, when I'm alone and singing one of the songs of Memphis, I try to remember the biblical stories of the strangers in strange lands—the biblical folks who left their homelands and made their homes in faraway, unfamiliar places. I try to remember how, though they missed home ("There's no place like home! There's no place like home!"), God helped them begin making a new home among a new people for His purposes. Remembering, I trust God is doing that with me, too.

Nevertheless, I can't help but think that if I ever get back to Memphis, I'm going to nail my feet to Beale Street!

Harry Potter and the Feckless Seminarian

2007. It's the year J. K. Rowling closed the books on our wonderful journeys into the always-magical realm of the Harry Potter stories. It also happens to be the year I closed the books on my wonderful journeys into the sometimes-mystical realm of theological education.

It took Ms. Rowling seventeen years and seven books to complete her wizard story. It took me sixteen years and three institutions to complete my seminary story. But the similarities don't just end there.

Young Harry Potter never fit in—always knowing he didn't belong—in the Dursleys' household. I wandered through two seminaries over several years, but never fit in and never belonged in either of them.

Then one day, like Hagrid arriving to deliver the news to young Harry that he is to attend the Hogwarts School of Witchcraft and Wizardry, a pastor/mentor told me I should attend a new seminary, the Baptist Seminary of Kentucky (BSK). Of course, Potter was eleven (and obviously single!) when he entered Hogwarts, whereas I was thirty-four and married (and with two young sons!) when my feet landed at BSK.

Providential (er . . . *magical*?) things happened that year—2002: BSK opened its doors for the first time; I matriculated that inaugural year; and I read *Harry Potter and the Sorcerer's Stone* for the first time.

During the ensuing years I immersed myself in the Harry Potter books (occasionally reading assigned seminary texts, too). The magical world in which Potter found a home, and in which he was undergoing great personal formation, mirrored the wonderful new seminary world in which I finally found a home and in which I, too, was undergoing great personal formation.

For example, Harry eventually came to terms with the house elves, Dobby and later Kreacher, who annoyed him greatly and initially made his life miserable. Over time Harry learned to appreciate them, love them, and trust them as close allies. Like Harry, during these seminary years I eventually came to terms with my own internal "house elf" of sorts—attention deficit disorder—which has annoyed me and made my life miserable for so long. However, I have learned to appreciate my ADD, love it, and trust it as a close ally. Also, like Harry's vulnerability to the dark, soul-sucking force of the Dementors, I learned to recognize and fight with the dark, soul-sucking force of clinical depression.

Hogwarts professors such as Lupin, Mad-Eye, McGonagall, and yes, even Snape, all kept watch over Harry and looked out for his well-being. BSK professors such as Drs. Adams, Hinson, Jackson, and Landon did the same for me. Harry was always under the watchful eye of Albus Dumbledore; and so Dr. Greg Earwood, the headmaster (er . . . *president*) of the Baptist Seminary of Kentucky, combined determination and boundless grace to make sure I both endured and graduated.

Of course, Harry had Ron, Hermione, and other close friends without whom he never would have survived. I, too, have my seminary friends (*you know who you are!*) without whom I never would have made it to the end.

So, 2007 marks the year that the final Harry Potter book was published, in which Harry Potter finally has a sense of who is and what his purpose is in life. And 2007 marks the year I graduated from seminary, in which I finally have a sense of who I am and who God is calling me to be.

I have shed tears knowing that I'll never read any new Harry Potter adventures, and knowing that I will never again sit as a student at the Baptist Seminary of Kentucky. But I anticipate returning to both Hogwarts and BSK again and again. All I have to do is open a book or jump in a car (oh, to have a flying Ford Anglia!).

Author's Assurance: Worry not—I have not developed some sort of twisted, messianic Potter complex. I am well aware that I am much more like a mixture of Ron Weasley, Luna Lovegood, and Rubeus Hagrid than anything resembling Mr. Potter.

Of Death, Dogs, and Davenports

I don't like most preachers. In fact, the more preachers I meet, the fewer preachers I like. This is ironic, since some of my best friends are preachers.

The Methodist preacher Jon Davenport was one of the good guys.

It's Easter Sunday morning, 2005. The cold, misty rain gently falls upon the faithful who gather for the annual Campbellsburg community sunrise service. Jon Davenport, being the newest preacher in town, is the chosen minister presiding over this early morning celebration.

Jon arrives early—*very early*. He builds a small fire around which we can gather and keep warm. He prepares the bread (a real, freshly baked loaf!) and the wine (or rather, juice—there will be Baptists present, too) for the faith community to share together in Holy Communion on this holiest of holy days.

Jon is a well-prepared pastor, delivering a well-prepared meditation, and about to officiate over a well-prepared observance of the Lord's Supper. But, as we huddle together around the warm fire, gathered under umbrellas and listening to Jon speak of the miracle of the day, a stray, scrappy dog sneaks up from behind, grabs the loaf of bread in his jaws, and runs a safe distance away where he promptly sits down and begins feasting on what was to be for us the body of Christ.

Jon completes his meditation and motions for me to hand him the bread, and I step forward and whisper the bad news. Jon blinks slowly, nods ever so slightly, and mumbles back at me in disbelief and resignation, "The dog . . . took . . . the bread."

Apart from this brief moment, though, Jon never loses his composure. A woman present has a small amount of wrapped banana-nut bread that was to be a gift for someone else, but she quietly offers it to Jon, who, as though this is exactly how he has scripted it, continues with great reverence and serves us the body and the blood of Christ.

This is pure 100 percent Jon Davenport.

Jon and I knew each other for a little more than three years. Jon and his family moved into the Campbellsburg Methodist parsonage one month after my family moved into the Campbellsburg Baptist parsonage. Jon and I were both seminary students at the time—he at Asbury Theological Seminary in Wilmore, Kentucky, and I at the Baptist Seminary of Kentucky in Lexington.

Initially, we compared classes, professors, assigned readings, and, of course, church experiences. We slowly discovered we had more in common than we ever imagined. We admired the same people: Stanley Hauerwas, Tex Sample, Jim Wallis, and Brian McLaren. We loved good rock and roll: Pearl Jam, Rush, Bruce Springsteen. He's also the only other preacher I knew who, like me, was inspired spiritually by *The X-Files*.

Jon, to me, was first a local ministerial colleague, but he soon grew to be a good friend, a trusted confidant, and, by the end of his brief stay in Campbellsburg, a brother. The latter, of course, solidified when Jon and his family moved into *our* parsonage for several days after the Methodist church exploded, damaging their parsonage.[1]

What could have been a stressed-out, overcrowded nightmare was one of the highlights of my life—and perhaps that of my whole family. The first ever Henry County Ecumenical Ministerial Commune, we called it. It seemed the eight of us couldn't get enough of each other.

Jon and his family soon moved to a Methodist church about an hour from us. We visited when we could, talked on the phone occasionally, and emailed often.

Then, Jon suddenly died from a rare fungal infection, blastomycosis, that seemed to eat away at his organs. He entered the hospital on a Monday, moved to intensive care on Thursday, and died on Saturday. Jon was thirty-six, and he left behind a wife and two young sons.

Jon, my ministerial colleague, my rock and roll comrade, my brother—our friendship was too short; our conversations too few; and our family get-togethers and late-night card games never enough, and *never* long enough. Like that dog on Easter Sunday morning, death came and snatched you away—when your friendship was providing so many of us with the sustenance of the Living Christ.

But thank you, Jon, for all you taught me, for all you shared and so freely gave of yourself, and for the memories that will walk with me forever.

Note

[1] There was a bizarre gas pipeline accident. Thanks be to God, absolutely nobody was physically injured, but the church building was reduced to rubble. Remember kids, "call before you dig"!

Why I'm a Political Cheerleader

There are three things we all know to be true: (1) the world would be at peace if only the Mississippi State Bulldogs (or occasionally the LSU Tigers) were national champions in *all* sports year after year; (2) the University of Tennessee Volunteers are the bane of all earthly existence; and (3) politics are a lot like collegiate sports.

I'm watching the 2008 presidential election like I just watched the NCAA basketball tournament. I have my favorite party (conference) and my favorite politicians (teams), and I cheer for them to win and move on when they lose. For example, I picked Mississippi State to make it all the way to the Final Four (and to win it all!), but had to settle for pulling for the Memphis Tigers instead after the Tigers knocked my Bulldogs out of the tournament.

Likewise, I've watched as presidential candidates, like my basketball Bulldogs, have been knocked out of the race one by one. Unlike my Bulldogs, though, my favorite candidate is still in the bracket to get to the White House.

I get a lot of flack from good friends and family members about how appalling my candidate is. To be fair, though, I have heard (and given) just as much flack about how despicable and dishonest the other candidates are. Some of these accusations from all sides are based in fact, though exaggerated; some are wild and goofy.

I decided long ago that if I waited for Jesus to come and be my perfect political candidate, I'd never vote again. So I tend to overlook nasty things if the good things appear to me to outweigh the bad . . . because let's face it, there's plenty of unsavory stuff to go around among all the candidates.

It's like college sports. If I waited for a team that emphasized its academics over its athletics and all of its players applied themselves first to their studies, well, I'd certainly never see many winning seasons (if any at all). Heck, my favorite team when I was growing up in New Orleans was the Tulane Green Wave. When it became known that their winning basketball team was cheating, Tulane University abolished its basketball program for several years! To be sure, if I'm going to have brain surgery and my surgeon played college sports, I'd want that surgeon to be a former Tulane player.[1]

Let's be honest: many of the big-name schools in national collegiate sports don't do well when it comes to graduation rates of their players. In my favorite conference alone, the Southeastern Conference, athletic programs have been caught providing tutors to write papers and take tests for players; providing money and cars and such to players and their families; even *buying* players from selected high schools! You can find all this and more just by searching the web. It's enough to make you decide never to watch collegiate sports again.

The religious Right can't stand John McCain. Hillary Clinton's campaign took cheap shots at Barack Obama. Obama's campaign found a polite way to go dirty in its responses to and charges against Clinton. The Republican party will pull out all the stops to defeat the Democrats, and the Democrats will pull out all the stops to outdo the Republicans. You can find all the disgusting dirt on any candidate and the parties' political practices just by searching the Web. It's enough to make you choose never to vote in any election ever again.

I know because I've tried giving up on both. But alas, I can't stay away from the thrills and excitement of Southeastern Conference sports; and I can't stay away from the thrills and excitement of big-time politics. So I've learned to turn a blind eye to all the awful dirt that goes with both in order to have some fun and, hopefully, make things a little bit better in our world. Besides, as I said earlier, if I waited for Jesus to be the quarterback of the Bulldogs, or Jesus to run for president of the United States, I'd never go to another game or voting booth again.

Yes, there are three things I know will bring lasting peace to the world: (1) a dominant Mississippi State Bulldog program in every sport (followed closely by the LSU Tigers); (2) the decline of the University of Tennessee Volunteers dominance in any sport; and (3) when my candidate is sworn in as the next president.

Or, maybe not. But nevertheless, I place my hope and trust in God through Jesus Christ, and I find a lot of joy cheering on my imperfect teams and imperfect politicians.

Note

[1] For the reasons I converted from being a Tulane fan to an LSU fan, see "Confessions of an LSU Convert (With Apologies to Mother)."

Epilogue

(Or, Elvis, Willie, Jesus and Me)

Sometime during 1976, Elvis Presley performed a concert in Baton Rouge, Louisiana. I was eight years old. We lived about an hour and a half away from Baton Rouge, and I begged—*pleaded!*—with my dad to take me to the Elvis concert. Dad, who unlike me was not a big Elvis fan, said firmly but lovingly, "Bert, Elvis has been around for twenty years; he'll be around for twenty more. You'll get to see him another time."

Elvis died the next year.

Like everyone else, I grieved. I doubled, I tripled, my efforts to buy all the Elvis records I could and watch all his movies when they were on television (even the gosh-awful most embarrassing ones). All the while, my parents continued listening to their favorite country music station.

Occasionally, I would hear a few songs on their station that grabbed my attention. They weren't my parents' favorite songs by any means, but they were being played on my parents' favorite radio station, and I liked them. Songs like "Good Hearted Woman," "Luchenbach, Texas (Back to the Basics of Love)," and "Mamas, Don't Let Your Babies Grow Up to Be Cowboys." I didn't know who sang them, but I knew they were great songs.

In 1979, Dad came home with a double album. It was a wild-looking album cover for Dad's standards, to be sure, but he loved some of the songs on that record. I admired the longhaired rebels pictured on the cover, and I immediately fell in love with all the music on the two LPs. It was Willie Nelson's duet album with rock legend Leon Russell, titled *One for the Road*. I soon learned that it was Willie Nelson, along with his old friend Waylon Jennings, who sang those other songs I liked hearing on my parents' favorite country station.

I continued my pursuit of all things Elvis, but began adding all things Willie, plus Waylon, then the Beatles, Led Zeppelin . . . you get the picture. Music has and still dominates my life. I know more about Ringo Starr than I do about George Washington; more about the Singing Nun than I do about the Nicene Creed and the Council of Trent combined.

I have also maintained a wrestling match with God. I struggle with God over all the nonsense we are allowed to do in God's name within "the church." I struggle with "the church" over all the things God is doing in the world despite our best efforts to deny it. I wrestle with Jesus over my will versus his lordship, and with following Jesus versus being a good churchy citizen. And I still hear the Holy Spirit whispering to me more often than not through the tragic life and great songs of Elvis Presley, not in the latest high-profile-let-me-sell-you-a-bunch-of-books-to-make-your-life-meaningful preacher of the month.

So, you see, I've always been at odds with, but can't break my connection to (for better or for worse!), the church. I am a church misfit. In some ways, all of these observations you are holding are glimpses of *my* gospel account. They represent *my* gospel story . . . the story of Elvis, Willie, Jesus, and me.